Brancusi
Gabo
Moholy-Nagy

Immaterial:

Kettle's Yard University of Cambridge
17 January - 14 March 2004
Southampton City Art Gallery
25 March - 23 May 2004

lenders:
Bauhaus Archiv, Berlin
Cabinet des estampes du Musée d'art et d'histoire, Geneva
Centre Georges Pompidou / Musée national d'art moderne, Paris
Institut Valencià d'Art Modern, Valencia
Hattula Moholy-Nagy
Musée Rodin, Paris
Museum Folkwang, Essen
Theodor Nicol
Private Collection
Tate, London
Nina and Graham Williams

catalogue designed by Paul Allitt
printed by Hilo Colour Printers Ltd, Colchester

ISBN 1 904561 04 7

This and other Kettle's Yard publications are available from
Kettle's Yard, Castle Street, Cambridge, CB3 0AQ
telephone 01223 352124 • www.kettlesyard.cam.ac.uk

front cover:
László Moholy-Nagy, Leda and the Swan, 1946, Cat. No. 57
back cover:
Constantin Brancusi, Leda, 1925-26, Cat. No. 17

foreword

Like humankind, sculpture aspires to defy and transcend its physical state.

Until the 20th century the great majority of Western sculpture was of the human figure. Carving in stone or wood, or modelling in clay and casting in bronze, the sculptor's task was to infuse dead matter with life. From Michelangelo to Rodin the gesture of the body, augmented by the creative gesture of the sculptor's hand, could suggest consciousness, thought and emotion. As Alberti observed approvingly in the 15th century: "The intellect moved and warmed by exercise becomes very *pronto* and quick in its work, and the hand follows speedily when a sure intellectual method leads it." It is interesting that this quality became valued at a time when sculptors began to draw and it is often in their drawings – rapid, two-dimensional, 'immaterial' – that we feel ourselves closest to the artist's aims.

This exhibition looks at the work of three 20th century sculptors who all came to work in the West from Eastern Europe and, arguably, were less rooted in the Italianate and Catholic tradition of life's energies being expressed in sculpture through muscle and sinew, whether described or describing. Brancusi's sculptures still speak of human beings and animals but the inner reflections, "the idea, the essence", of Prometheus or the darting movement of a fish are the result of light on a honed surface instead of any naturalistic simulation. Gabo's first stereometric constructions were of heads and torsos, without their body mass, but soon his sculptures were exploring space and time as such, in parallel with contemporary science and aided by new, man-made materials. Their transparencies were also adopted by Moholy-Nagy who moved freely among sculpture, painting, graphic work, photography and film, calling himself a 'manipulator of light'.

Photography, light's own medium, appears to play an important part. The exhibition begins with photographs which Rodin had taken of his sculptures, some, tellingly, by his patinator who would have understood the exact effects the sculptor sought. Brancusi photographed his own sculptures and, in doing so, showed light as his active collaborator. Moholy, seeing photography as "one of the most important factors in the dawn of a new life", used objects to make photograms and filmed the light reflections and shadows cast by his kinetic construction, the Light-Space Modulator. We even find that Gabo made photographs of moving light, suggestive of forms which had or would appear in his sculpture.

Light, space, time and movement – all that sculpture was not – were now its subject and its media.

Michael Harrison, Director

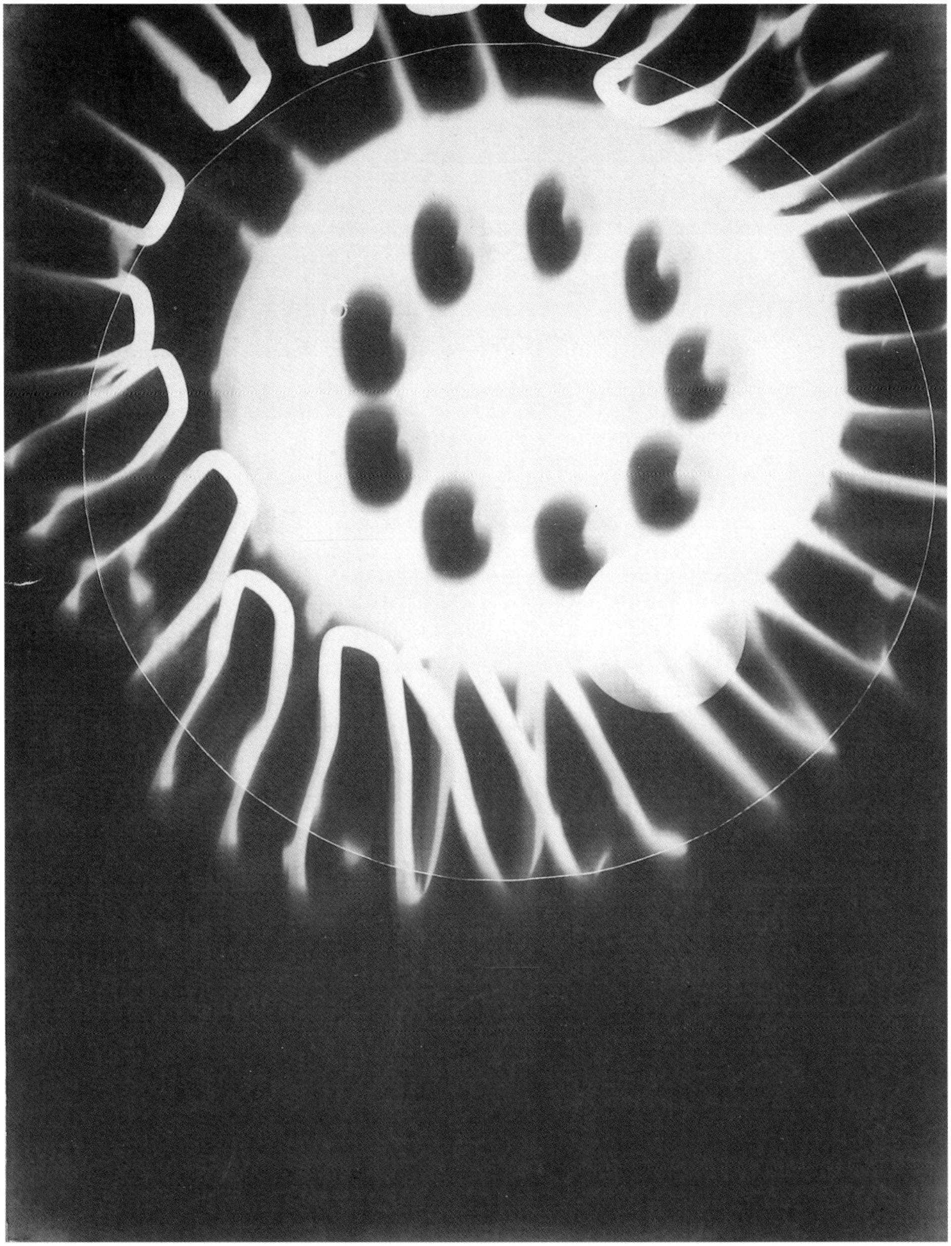

László Moholy-Nagy
Untitled photogram
1925-28 Cat. No. 51

NEW VISIONS FOR A NEW WORLD

Sebastiano Barassi

The development of radically new philosophical and scientific ideas in the late 19th and early 20th century had a dramatic impact on the ways in which the world was perceived. A fundamental challenge to the objectivity of philosophical and scientific knowledge came in the 1880s from Friedrich Nietzsche, who ridiculed what he called the doctrine of 'immaculate perception' and invoked a 're-evaluation of all values'. Soon after, Henri Bergson (who is regarded as 'the artist's philosopher' for his influence on much early 20th century art) affirmed the supremacy of intuition over intellect, expressing the aspiration to take philosophy out of the speculative and into the spiritual sphere, to provide it with foundations distinct from those of science. Interestingly, both philosophers questioned the dominance of sight over the other senses, commencing an attack on ocularcentrism which was to be echoed in the work of, amongst others, Marcel Proust and the Gestaltists.

Further emphasis on the inadequacy of direct experience for the exploration of natural phenomena came with the publication of Albert Einstein's theory of relativity (1905) and Ernest Rutherford's model of the atomic structure (1909-11), which depicted a universe that could no longer be fully understood simply through the senses. At this point the gap between the images of the world presented by scientists and philosophers and that derived from everyday experience was wider than it had ever been. Predictably, this had a dramatic impact on the arts which found it increasingly more difficult to rely on their traditional languages to represent the new world that was emerging. Naum Gabo described this state of uncertainty in 1937, when, looking back on the early years of the century, he wrote that "the edifice of Art as well as the edifice of Science was undermined and corroded by a spirit of fearless analysis which ended in a revolutionary explosion."[1] The artist recalled that it was then that the word 'impossibility' disappeared from the lexicon of science and a much more intangible image of reality took shape.

Technological progress also played a key role in this perceptual shift. Electric light and apparatuses, systems to record and reproduce sound and, above all, photography all had a dramatic impact on the ways of seeing and representing reality. Particularly significant for the visual arts was the invention of photography. Soon after its appearance in the 1830s, the new medium was universally hailed as a 'faithful mirror' of reality and an objective documentary tool. In this sense, photography had both a positive and a negative influence on the artistic developments that followed its appearance. On the one hand, it deposed painting as the medium endorsed for the task of documenting reality faithfully. On the other hand, the views it could offer through its many applications were so innovative and striking that it became a source of inspiration for many new pictorial and sculptural languages. Aerial images, microphotography, radiography, chronophotography (the meticulous dissection of movement in parts individually undetectable by the human eye) and, most importantly, the moving image, offered such innovative insights into reality to make Lászlό Moholy-Nagy exclaim in 1925: "through a hundred years of photography and two decades of film ... we see the world with entirely different eyes."[2]

The First World War, with its fierce trench warfare and unprecedented loss of life, also had a major impact on the perception of the world of those who witnessed it, undermining established value systems and even affecting visual experience. Martin Jay has suggested that the war "created a bewildering landscape of indistinguishable, shadowy shapes, illuminated by lightning flashes of blinding intensity, and then obscured by phantasmagoric, often gas-induced haze ... When all that the soldiers could see was the sky above and the mud below, the traditional reliance on visual evidence for survival could no longer be easily maintained."[3]

1. Naum Gabo, "The Constructive Idea in Art", in J.L. Martin, B. Nicholson and N. Gabo (Eds.), *Circle*, London 1937 (1971 edition, p. 5).
2. L. Moholy-Nagy, *Malerei, Fotografie, Film*, Munich 1925 (translation by J. Seligman, *Painting, Photography, Film*, Cambridge, Mass., 1969, p. 29)
3. M. Jay, *Downcast Eyes*, Berkeley 1993, pp. 212-13

Not surprisingly, artists were quick to respond to the new reality that was appearing before their eyes. In particular, but with the degree of generalisation necessary in a short essay, it seems plausible to describe the technological, scientific and philosophical evolution which revolutionised the vision of the world as a key factor in the development of a non-representational art. This was, in some of its manifold manifestations, a blunt statement of the inadequacy of traditional artistic languages to understand and reorder the new reality, and it was, in fact, often accompanied by a nihilistic proclamation of the death of the 'old' art.[4] Significantly, many of the artists experimenting with the new languages refused the label 'abstract' for their art, emphasising that is was to be intended in a wider sense, as a representation of invisible realities or, as Gabo defined it, an alternative form of realism.[5]

The ways in which artists expressed their changing relationship with the universe were, of course, extremely varied. Some, like the Suprematists, Wassily Kandinsky, or Constantin Brancusi, were interested in investigating spiritual or 'absolute' ideas. Others, like Gabo, Moholy-Nagy and the Constructivists, moved from a materialist – and often utopian – faith in modernity and technology, to creating an art which would be an integral part of the new reality and could contribute to the improvement of society and the birth of a 'new man'. The aesthetics that developed from these researches were inevitably of a very different nature. It is possible, however, to identify common interests and strategies across the spectrum of early Modernism. One of these is the fascination with the dematerialisation of pictorial and sculptural forms as a response to the perceived dematerialisation of value systems and of the physical world. This, in its manifestations in the work of Constantin Brancusi, Naum Gabo and László Moholy-Nagy, is the theme of the present exhibition.

4. László Moholy-Nagy wrote in *Malerei, Fotografie, Film* (cit., p. 45) that "traditional painting has become a historical relic and is finished with. Eyes and ears have been opened and are filled at every moment with a wealth of optical and phonetic wonders. A few more vitally progressive years ... and it will be a matter of universal knowledge that photography was one of the most important factors in the dawn of a new life."

5. Gabo insisted on the realism of his art, and entitled his first major statement on Constructivism *The Realistic Manifesto*. As he explained in *Abstraction-Création* in 1932: "A work of constructivist art is under no circumstances an abstraction. We do not turn away from nature but on the contrary, we penetrate it more profoundly than naturalistic art would ever be able to do." (republished in M. Hammer and C. Lodder, Eds., *Gabo on Gabo*, East Sussex 2000, p. 83). Similarly, Brancusi declared that "there are fools who call my work abstract. What they think to be abstract is the most realistic, because what is real is not the outer form, but the idea, the essence of things." (quoted by C. Gilles Guilbert, "Propos de Brancusi", in *Prisme des Artes*, no. 12, 1957, p. 6; my translation).

The concept of dematerialisation applied to the visual arts is wide-ranging and often vague. Martin Hammer and Christina Lodder present a definition and an analysis of its implications in their essay. Indeed, the interest in achieving dematerialised effects in art pre-dated the work of the three artists in this exhibition. The diffusion of photography in the second half of the 19th century gave impulse to the development of new aesthetics in painting and sculpture, which were based primarily on the questioning of traditional perspectival construction, on a renewed interest in colour and light and on the desire to create visual effects similar to those seen in photographic images. From the 1870s, for instance, Impressionism attempted to translate into painting and sculpture the blurred images and flattened space of the new medium. With their characteristic freshness of representation and loose brushwork, artists like Claude Monet (whose late, almost abstract water lily paintings are paradigmatic in this sense) were inspired by photography to rediscover the power of light as an essential pictorial element. Building on these premises, and always remaining within the realm of naturalistic two-dimensional art, the Impressionists' success was the consequence of their approach to representation with the intent to present their own 'impression' rather than an accurate rendition of reality.

A significant early example of the investigation into dematerialising effects is offered by the drawings of Auguste Rodin (1840-1917) and the photography of his sculpture, and arguably even by the sculpture itself. From the 1870s Rodin's ink sketches and watercolours revealed an interest in exploring very dynamic and ethereal effects. If, on the one hand, this is in harmony with his investigation into the representation of movement and the powerful emotional character of his sculpture, on the other it seems to be in sharp contrast with the solidity and weight of most of his three-dimensional output. Rodin only rarely used drawing as a preparatory tool, and instead considered the medium a quick way of observing existing sculpture and recording his most intimate visual concerns. In this sense, the visionary and dematerialised nature of many of his drawings seems the result of his way of looking ('the vision of the sculptor', as he labelled a sketch of 1883) rather than an objective record. The feel of immateriality and weightlessness is particularly strong in the sculptor's late watercolours, which feature figures without a background, almost floating on the page, and extraordinary effects of transparency achieved through the subtle use of washes. Two-dimensional images, however, could also help Rodin to emphasise the weightiness of a piece. The photographs of

Ugolino that he commissioned from E. Freuler in c.1877,[6] for instance, show the figure looking more like a monolith than a human, using the mass of the sculpture as a visual metaphor of the moral weight of Ugolino's Dantean torment.

Indeed, photography played a very important role in Rodin's investigation into sculpture and its presentation, as discussed in detail by Geraldine A. Johnson in her essay. The images commissioned by the artist are mainly concerned with the suggestive use of natural light. Rodin had a predilection for studying sculpture by candlelight, and, as shown by Eugène Druet's photographs of the **Age of Bronze** (c.1898; cat nos. 1 and 2) and **Eve** (c.1899; cat. nos. 3 and 4) he asked his photographers to use a single light source, preferably a narrow window set high in the wall, for dramatic effect. An even more emotional use of dematerialising effects is found in the photographs of the **Burghers of Calais** (c.1908; cat nos. 5-7) commissioned by Rodin from Jean-François Limet, a *patinateur* (the craftsman responsible for the patination of bronze) who worked in his studio. These ghostly, soft-focus images are remarkably similar to the paintings of Rodin's friend Eugène Carrière and were made with the gum bichromate technique.[7] This allowed a treatment of the figures of the 14th century city leaders, here seen going to their sacrifice to lift the siege of the city, making them look like ghosts, or the damned souls found in Rodin's sketchbooks. Interestingly, though, a surface treatment which is surprisingly suggestive of the patination process gives the photographs a very strong physical presence, with an ambiguity between two and three-dimensional which is not uncommon in Rodin.

The photographs of Rodin's sculpture show a concern with formal dematerialisation for clearly expressive purposes. In this they are closer to 19th century spirit photography than to the use of similar effects that were by then developing in some avant-garde circles. From around 1907, Cubism initiated a radical attack against traditional pictorial and sculptural languages, declaring that the representation of the real should no longer be based on perspectival constructions and a single, fixed viewpoint, but on multiple, and simultaneous, views. This led to the creation of a characteristic language founded on fragmentation, deconstruction and

6. See C. Lampert, *Rodin: Sculpture and Drawing*, London 1986, pl. 30.
7. The gum bichromate process was introduced at the end of the 19th century. It enables one to alter tones, obliterate details, and, by using a brush, pencil or rubber, to rework an image in order to make it look more like a painting or a charcoal drawing.

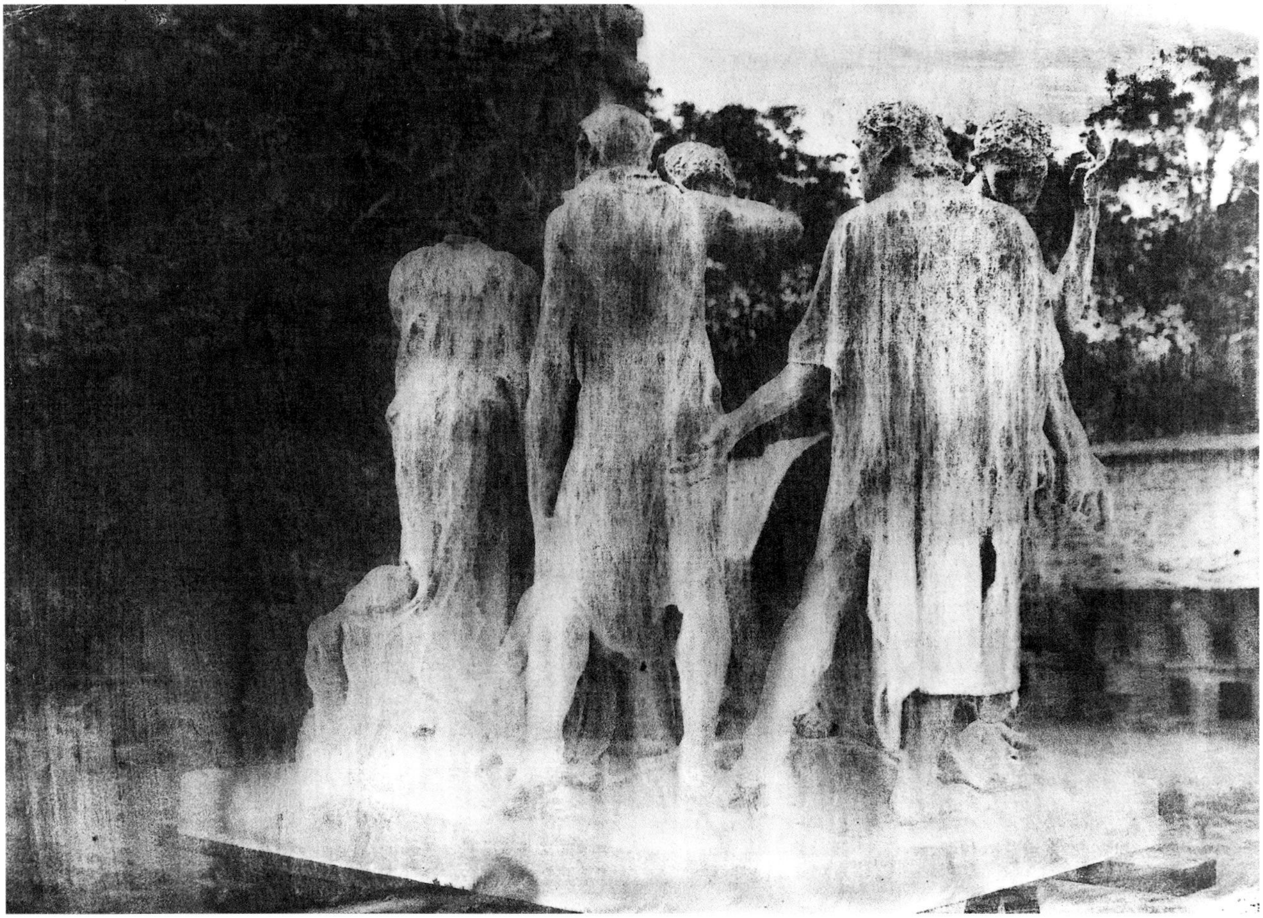

Jean-François Limet
Le Monument aux Bourgeois de Calais
(The Burghers of Calais) Cat. No. 7

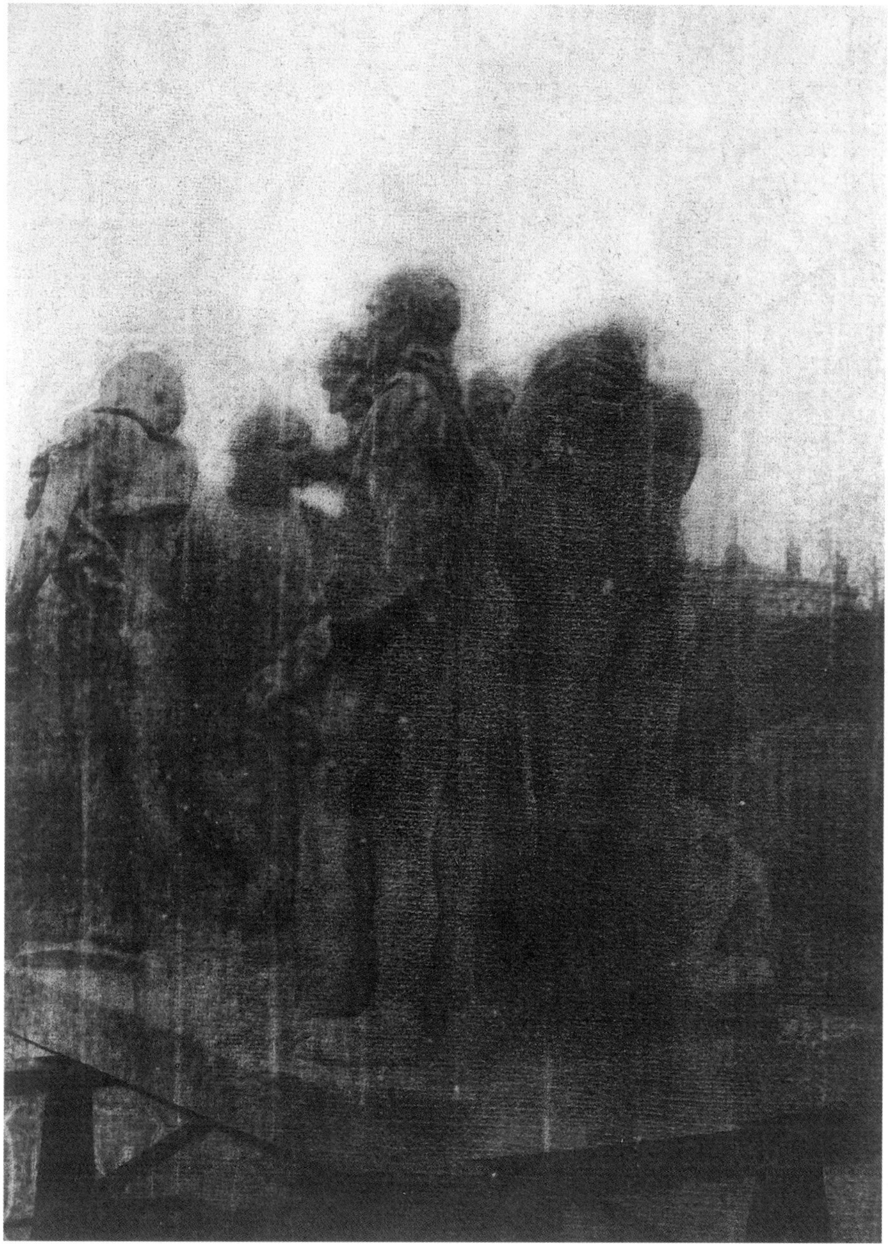

Jean-François Limet
Le Monument aux Bourgeois de Calais
(The Burghers of Calais) Cat. No. 5

rearrangement of forms in intricate compositions of planes, which, for the first time, acknowledged the inadequacy of sight for a full understanding of reality.[8] With Cubism art entered the final phase of disintegration of pictorial and sculptural space which, although not necessarily a direct response to new scientific and philosophical ideas, was the first manifestation of that *zeitgeist*.

In the early 1910s Futurism introduced into art the study of two interrelated elements which would contribute decisively to the creation of effects of dematerialisation: movement and time. Inspired by the experiments with chronophotography and moving images, the Futurists promoted an aesthetic which glorified the dynamism of modern urban life. This stimulated a research into the mechanics of movement which became one of their trademarks. Despite its freshness and originality, Futurist painting somehow failed to achieve a truly dynamic representation of movement. Sculpture, however, was much more successful and subtle in its approach. In his 1912 *Technical Manifesto of Futurist Sculpture*, Umberto Boccioni (1882-1916) theorised the introduction of rhythm and dynamism in the plastic arts through the use of 'force-lines' and modern materials such as glass, electric light and motors. Boccioni died prematurely, and his innovative ideas remained on paper only. His insistence on experimenting with movement in sculpture, however, especially when compared with the results achieved by contemporary painting, seems to indicate that three-dimensional art was already seen as more likely to succeed in expressing the new visual concerns of the artists who wanted to respond to the changing vision of the world.

This became evident with Constructivism, the first movement openly to express a fundamental concern with the use of dematerialised effects in sculpture. Originated in Russia around 1914 with the work of Vladimir Tatlin (1885-1953), Constructivism promoted a politicised and socially-oriented approach, based on a blind faith in technology and a utilitarian view of art as the means to create a new

8. As Moholy-Nagy later remarked, Cubism began "to peel off the surfaces of the object, to disintegrate it, in order to become fully acquainted with its structural elements." (L. Moholy-Nagy, *The New Vision and Abstract of an Artist*, New York 1947, p. 35). Gabo added that "instead of taking the object as a separate world and passing it through his perceptions producing a third object, namely the picture, which is the product of the first two, the Cubist transfers the entire inner world of his perceptions with all its component parts (logic, emotion and will) into the interior of the object penetrating through its whole structure, stretching its substance to such an extent that the outside integument explodes and the object itself appears destroyed and unrecognizable." (Naum Gabo, *The Constructive Idea in Art*, cit., p. 4).

society. During the 1920s Constructivism became a widely spread international movement. Its ideas circulated throughout Europe, thanks to the migrations of artists like Moholy-Nagy and Gabo, and with the crucial support of publications like *Der Sturm* (which, in 1922, published Moholy-Nagy's and Alfréd Kemény's manifesto *The Constructive Dynamic System of Forces)* and *G: Material zur elementaren Gestaltung* (1923-26). Across its local reinterpretations, Constructivism put varying emphasis on different ideological aspects, acquiring a surprisingly wide range of nuances. Its key aesthetic elements, however, remained the concern with the introduction of real space, movement and time in sculpture and the use of industrial materials (glass, plastic, standardised metal parts) in constructions with clear formal arrangements.

Because of its very nature, Constructivism had close links with contemporary architectural trends investigating the use of glass and transparency.[9] Ludwig Mies van der Rohe's projects of the early 1920s for glass skyscrapers and his German Pavilion for the International Exhibition in Barcelona (1929) are among the most significant examples of the new aesthetic value attributed to light, translucency and reflections in architecture. Emerging in Germany in the aftermath of the First World War, this interest was partly a consequence of the technical developments which now allowed glass to be used for construction purposes. In this sense, Walter Gropius' 1919 proclamation of glass as the 'crystal symbol of the new faith of the future', which was echoed in the functionalist theories of Adolf Behne, shows how transparency and light had become a lucid architectural ideal. However, the fascination with light was also at the heart of the search for expressionistic effects outlined by Paul Scheerbart in his seminal book *Glasarchitektur* (1913), which formulated a theory of glass in architecture with highly spiritual and almost mystical implications.

9. Close collaboration between artists and architects characterised many publications and groups of the 1920s and 30s: the Bauhaus, *G*, *Unit One* and *Circle*, to name only a few. The fruits of these interactions can be found in Naum Gabo's 'columns' and 'towers' from the early 1920s, which have a strong architectural feel. Gabo also worked with actual architecture (he submitted a project for the Palace of the Soviets in Moscow, in 1931) and had links with progressive architects such as Ludwig Mies van der Rohe and Hannes Meyer. Perhaps more surprisingly, an architectural interest informs Brancusi's work: in addition to the monumental complex at Tirgu-Jiu, his plan to turn *Endless Column* into a 400-metre high building in polished steel is well documented, as are his fascination with Le Corbusier's ideas and the many visits paid by architects to his studio. Interestingly, Issue 4 of G magazine featured images of Mies' Friedrichstraße project alongside Brancusi's own photograph of *Bird in Space*.

The manifold attitudes towards the use of glass and transparency in architecture demonstrate how the interest in dematerialising effects spanned several different strands of Modernism, and could even be regarded as a *fil rouge* that unites them. This exhibition explores how this shared interest informed the work of three artists who had otherwise rather diverse aesthetic agendas, and whose grouping here does not imply any suggestion of a broader artistic homogeneity. All three were of Eastern European origin: Constantin Brancusi (1876-1957) was Romanian, Naum Gabo (1890-1977) Russian and László Moholy-Nagy (1894-1946) Hungarian. And all three, albeit for different reasons, left their native countries relatively early in their lives to pursue a career abroad. Dematerialisation, however, was not their sole artistic concern. The majority of Brancusi's output, in fact, consists of very material works carved in wood and stone. Naum Gabo, discussing Constructivism, wrote that "we are not at all intending to dematerialise a sculptural work, making it non-existent, we are realists, bound to earthly matters."[10] And Moholy-Nagy's approach was deeply materialist in nature, regarding design – not sculpture – as the art form that could truly contribute to the progress of mankind. It is also worth mentioning, here, that other contemporary artists, Georges Vantongerloo above all, showed an interest in dematerialised sculpture. However, in their own different ways Brancusi, Gabo and Moholy showed a determination and a thoroughness in exploring the possibilities offered by the use of real space, movement, time and light in sculpture, which were not matched by any other artist from that generation.

The three had clearly different motives for investigating concepts of dematerialisation. Unlike Gabo and Moholy, both prolific writers, Brancusi was generally reluctant to discuss his work, and his thoughts have mostly been recorded by others in the form of brief aphorisms known as *propos*. In one of these, "Mais la sculpture, c'est de l'eau, de l'eau,"[11] the artist likened sculpture to water. This seems a fitting metaphor for his vision of the medium as based upon reflection and transparency, in constant movement and capable of metamorphosing in different states.[12] A similarly suggestive insight into Brancusi's art is offered by one of the

10. N. Gabo, "Sculpture: Carving and Construction in Space", in J.L. Martin, B. Nicholson and N. Gabo, *op. cit.*, p. 108.
11. Quoted in S. Geist, *Brancusi*, New York 1968, p. 164.
12. Perhaps not surprisingly, the idea of using water appealed to all three artists. Both Gabo and Brancusi worked on projects for fountains (Brancusi's *Narcissus Fountain* of 1914; and Gabo's *Revolving Torsion, Fountain* of 1972-3 in London, or the project for a *Rotating Fountain* of c.1925), while Moholy-Nagy considered water an ideal artistic medium (which he explored in the amusing documentary *The Life of Lobsters* of 1936).

central themes of his sculpture, flight. The artist, who had witnessed the achievements of the pioneers of aviation, made numerous works inspired by flight, which for him represented a metaphor for the search for spiritual elevation with which his art was concerned.[13] From this point of view, his tendency to develop virtually all of his bird series in the direction of increasingly slimmer and more elongated, evanescent forms, signals a movement from the material to the immaterial, and from the profane to the sacred associated with the theme of flight. Here Brancusi reveals his fundamentally Neo-Platonic disposition, which was at the foundation of his search for an art representing not a visible reality but what he called 'the essence of things'. This search for archetypal images resulted in the extreme simplification of forms characteristic of his sculptures. The use of dematerialising effects, in this respect, served to enhance the perception of the works as images of a higher order, above the physical world. In this, he was influenced not only by Greek philosophy but also by theories of science relating to energy and vibration (Brancusi's fascination with the theories of Bergson and Poincaré is well documented) and an interest in esotericism and theosophy.

Unlike the Romanian, Gabo was less inclined to attribute a purely spiritual value to his art, preferring to emphasise its nature of investigation into a reality that required new ways of seeing, which made it an apt tool for the improvement of society. From this point of view, his interest in an aesthetic rich in dematerialising effects was motivated by the need for an art that was to reflect and understand a world "in which forces are permitted to become mass and matter is permitted to become light."[14] In spite of his stressing the fundamental realism and utilitarianism of his approach, however, Gabo was eager to clarify that his constructions were not a mere illustration of scientific ideas. While he believed that both the artist and the scientist are prompted by the same creative urge to find a perceptible image of the hidden forces of nature and to favour the advancement of mankind, he was also keen to underline the differences in their approach: "Science teaches, explores, comprehends, reasons and proves. Art asserts, art acts, art makes believe."[15] Some

13. Mircea Eliade (in *Témoignages sur Brancusi*, Paris 1967, p. 93) reported Brancusi as saying: "all my life I have looked for nothing but the essence of flight ... Flight, that's happiness!" (my translation). Brancusi was an avid reader of the *Book of Milarepa*, the story of an 11th century Tibetan monk who acquired the power to change his body into any shape and to fly across the sky like a bird, a fascination which is emblematic of the sculptor's own aspiration to the sublime.
14. N. Gabo, *On Constructive Realism*, 1948 (republished in M. Hammer and C. Lodder, *op. cit.*, p. 171).
15. Id., "The Constructive Idea in Art", in J.L. Martin, B. Nicholson and N. Gabo, *op. cit.*, p. 8.

of Gabo's lectures are enlightening from this point of view.[16] In them he explained that he was not at all interested in eliminating the 'irrational spirit' from art, and that Constructivism

> realised that it was possible to find the complete irrationality of the Absolute in a piece of wood, in the transparent quality of the material of a piece of glass, in the corporeal reality of a stone, in the heaviness of iron, in the floating lightness of air, in the vibration of light ... We [the Constructivists] drew this conviction of ours from the (after all so) rational sources of exact science and this conviction gave us courage to make demands, to build pictorial art on the basis of the same real laws on which our entire world ... is built. For in these laws, however real and rational they might appear, we felt that the highest spiritual potential of the irrational was revealed.[17]

Like Gabo's, Moholy's approach was fundamentally utilitarian, especially early in his career, when he professed his faith in the cult of the machine and mass-production[18] and stressed the role of design as a complex system, integral to everyday life, for seeing and interpreting reality. However, in later years the artist progressively abandoned his 'technological monomania', in an attempt to put more emphasis on the human element in the industrial age.[19] A crucial role in this shift was played by what has been described as his 'mysticism of light', which allowed him to unite in a coherent vision the eulogy of modern technology as an untiring provider of energy with a mystique of light and the immaterial that was rooted in the deepest psychological needs of mankind. Eventually, it was this interest that led Moholy to investigate the possibilities of dematerialisation in art.

16. Id., *The Rational and Irrational in Modern Art*, Berlin 1930 (republished in M. Hammer and C. Lodder, *op cit.*, pp. 65-70); Id., *Of Divers Arts*, Washington D.C. 1959.
17. Id., *The Rational and Irrational in Modern Art*, cit., p. 70.
18. As early as 1922 Moholy expressed his desire "to go beyond vanity into the realm of objective validity, serving the public as an anonymous agent ... I was not afraid of losing the 'personal touch', so highly valued in previous painting ... I even gave up signing my paintings. I put numbers and letters with the necessary data on the back of the canvas, as if they were cars, aeroplanes, or other industrial products" (L. Moholy-Nagy, *The New Vision*, cit., p. 79). Moholy famously produced a series of 'telephone paintings' in porcelain enamel commissioned by telephone from a factory, giving details of colours and forms sketched on graph paper over the phone, without participating in the physical production of the works. At this time, his approach was close to the Productivist ideas of the artist-engineer and the mechanical mass-production of art.
19. Moholy championed the replacement of the idea of *Gesamtkunstwerk* (the total work of art as intended by De Stijl and the early Bauhaus) with that of *Gesamtwerk* (life itself), an all-embracing creativity born out of individual necessity to become universal (see *Malerei, Fotografie, Film*, cit., p. 17).

Regardless of their differences in approach, the three artists sought to achieve formal dematerialisation in their work through the use of similar principles, namely the introduction of new ideas of space, time, movement and light, the challenge to the traditional concept of balance and the rejection of the reliance on sight as the privileged sense for the investigation of reality.

At the core of the research of all three artists is the discourse on space and volume, which was closely linked with their shared desire to end illusionism in art and led them to question sculpture's traditional reliance on solid mass. The writings of both Gabo and Moholy-Nagy, which defined the guiding principles of Constructivism, put much emphasis on this. The Russian, who had trained as a scientist and was well aware of the latest theoretical developments, specified that space was not merely a philosophical or scientific principle at the foundation of a new aesthetic, but a completely concrete and real sculptural element, "what colour has meant to a painter and clay to the sculptor."[20] Moholy agreed, and explained that one of the chief aims of Constructivism was "a new space created with light directly."[21]

Both artists believed that the way to introduce space in sculpture was through the dissolution of its physical boundary, the surface. Gabo's first response to this problem was the elaboration of the 'stereometrical method', in the mid-1910s. He adopted it for a series of figurative constructions he made in Norway around 1915-17, one of which is the **Model for 'Constructed Torso'** (1917; cat no. 24) in the exhibition. Here volume is not defined by surfaces but through intersecting planes which show the space in which mass exists, rather than mass itself. This technique would soon be replaced by the use of transparent planes, which is described in detail by Martin Hammer and Christina Lodder in their essay. Partly inspired by Gabo's example, Moholy too investigated the possibility of dissolving sculptural surfaces visually through the adoption of translucent materials. However, as discussed later, the focus of his research became the use of real light, and the Hungarian subsequently treated sculpture as one of the various media available to modulate it.

20. N. Gabo, *The Problems of Space and Time and Their Falsification*, 1925 (republished in C. Lodder and M. Hammer, *op. cit.*, p. 41).
21. L. Moholy-Nagy, *The New Vision*, cit., p. 39.

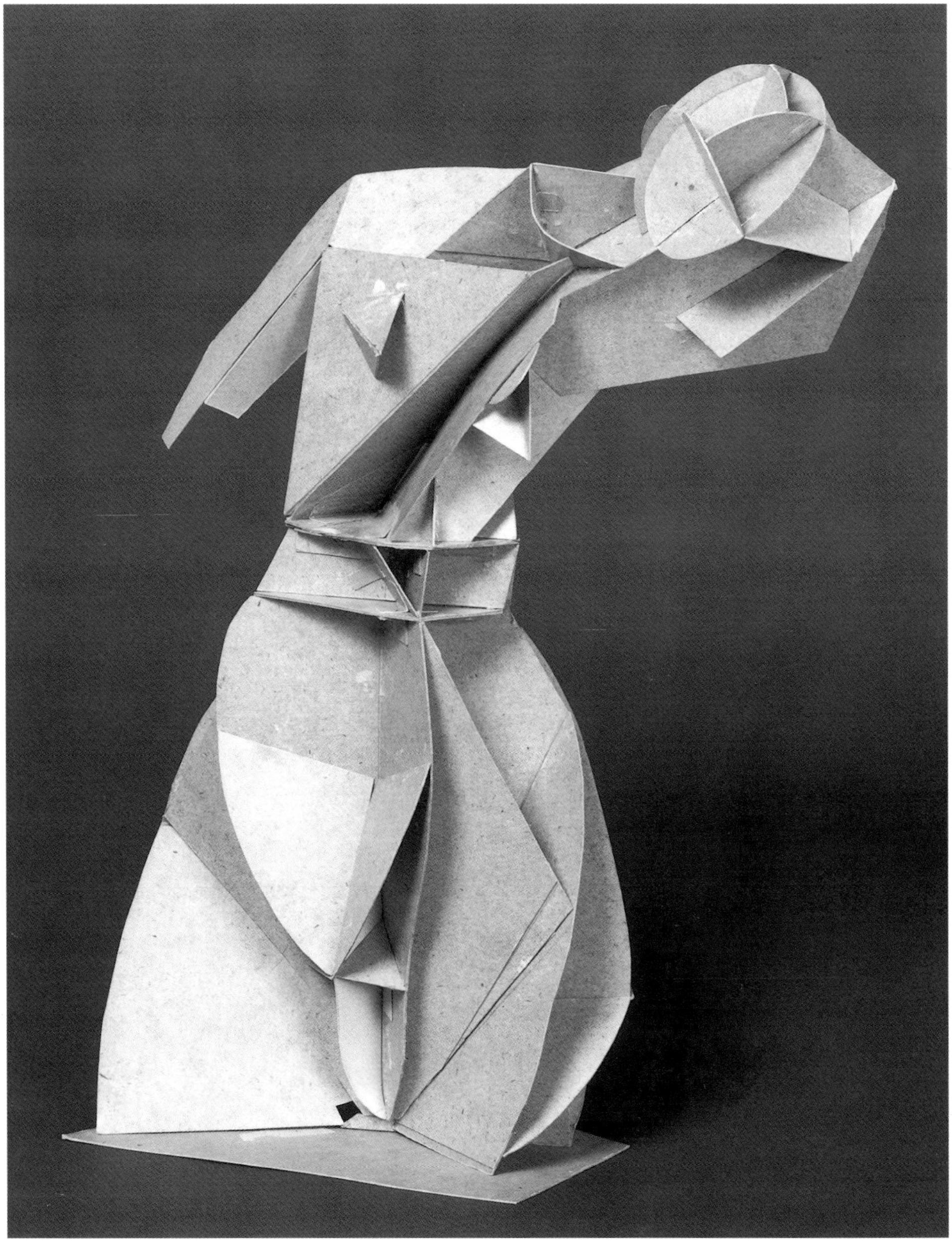

Naum Gabo
Model for 'Constructed Torso'
1917 (reassembled 1981) Cat. No. 24

Brancusi too was interested in creating works which would not be understood from their surfaces but as pure volumes. His search for extreme formal simplification was informed by a very Oriental sense of the 'void'. This inspired the artist, who expressed his dislike of Michelangelo's earthly figures, to attempt to lighten the weight and solidity of sculptural mass by animating the surface with subtle spatial and dynamic effects. Brancusi's determination to pursue a weightless and dematerialised sculpture was such that, in the 1930s, he destroyed some of his wood and stone carvings and abandoned the use of pierced forms, dissatisfied with the sense of solidity created by the shadows in the holes. The sculptor, in associating shadow with heavy mass and weight, attributed to its opposite, light, a sense of physical and metaphysical 'lightness'. The modulation of light on the surface, in this sense, became for Brancusi a crucial strategy, which allowed him to achieve some of his most striking results in terms of dematerialisation.

The role of light and its modulation was, in fact, central not only in the creation but also in the presentation of the work of all three artists. Their research revolved around a use of light which was fundamentally different from the illusionistic effects of earlier impressionistic art: here were actual optical phenomena created by real light in space, not just their two-dimensional representation.

Brancusi explored different strategies to use light to dissolve the surface of his works. In the sculpture itself, as early as 1905 he began to make highly polished bronze pieces, and by 1912 this had became a customary technique. Shiny surfaces allowed him to create effects with both reflecting and emanating light and to include the surrounding environment and movement in the sculpture, occasionally exploiting mesmerising multiplication effects. Both **Leda** and **Fish** (cat. nos. 10 and 11), for instance, sit on polished metal discs, which reflect the surrounding environment and the sculptures themselves, which in turn reflect the discs and their reflections, and so on. Even when using less obviously reflecting materials, as in the case of the cement version of **Prometheus** (cat. no. 8), Brancusi adopted techniques like surface polishing and the inclusion of metal dust in the mix to achieve similarly fascinating, though much more subtle, light effects.

The use of reflections, however, had its drawbacks. The presentation of the sculptures was more difficult to control, with the surroundings and any movement being picked up by the reflective surfaces. Unlike his friend Duchamp, Brancusi was

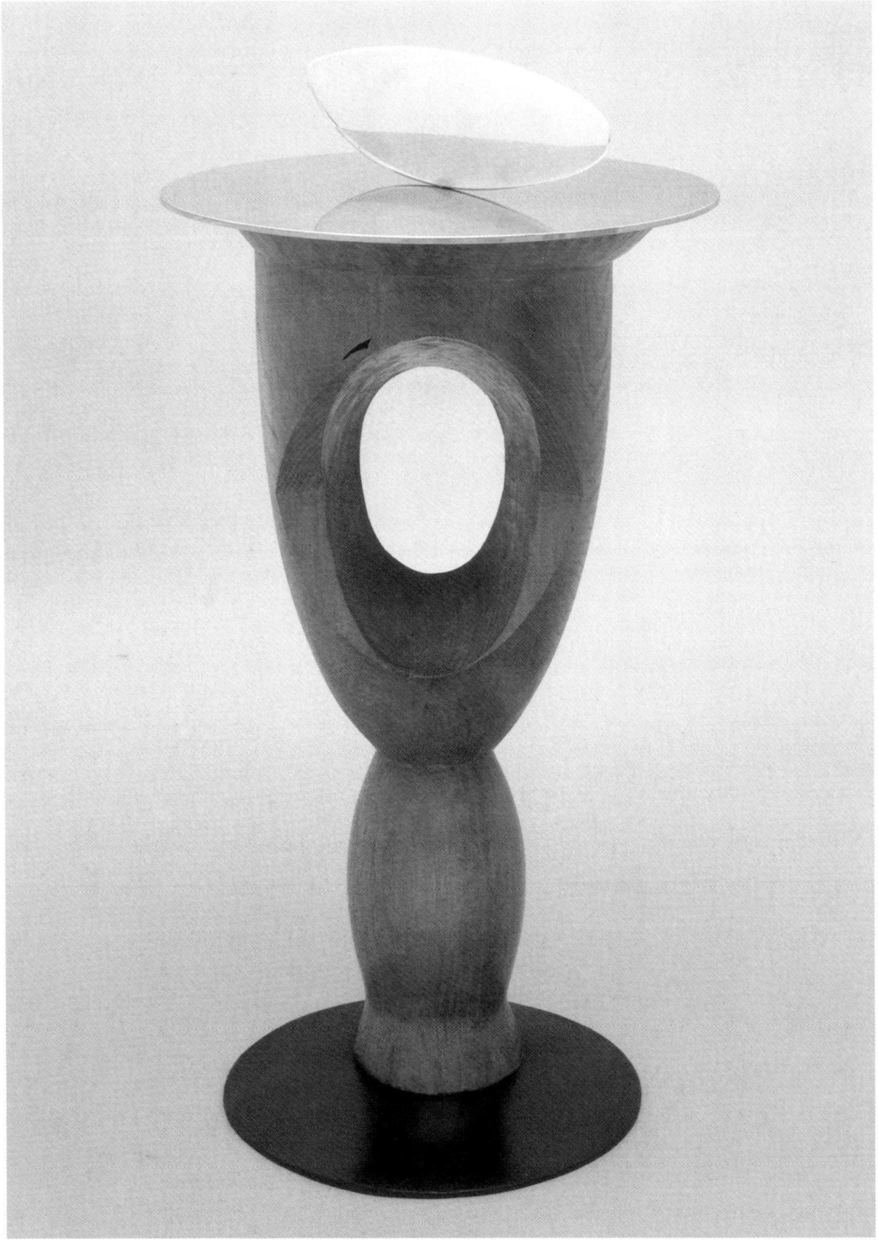

Constantin Brancusi
Poisson (Fish)
1926 Cat. No. 11

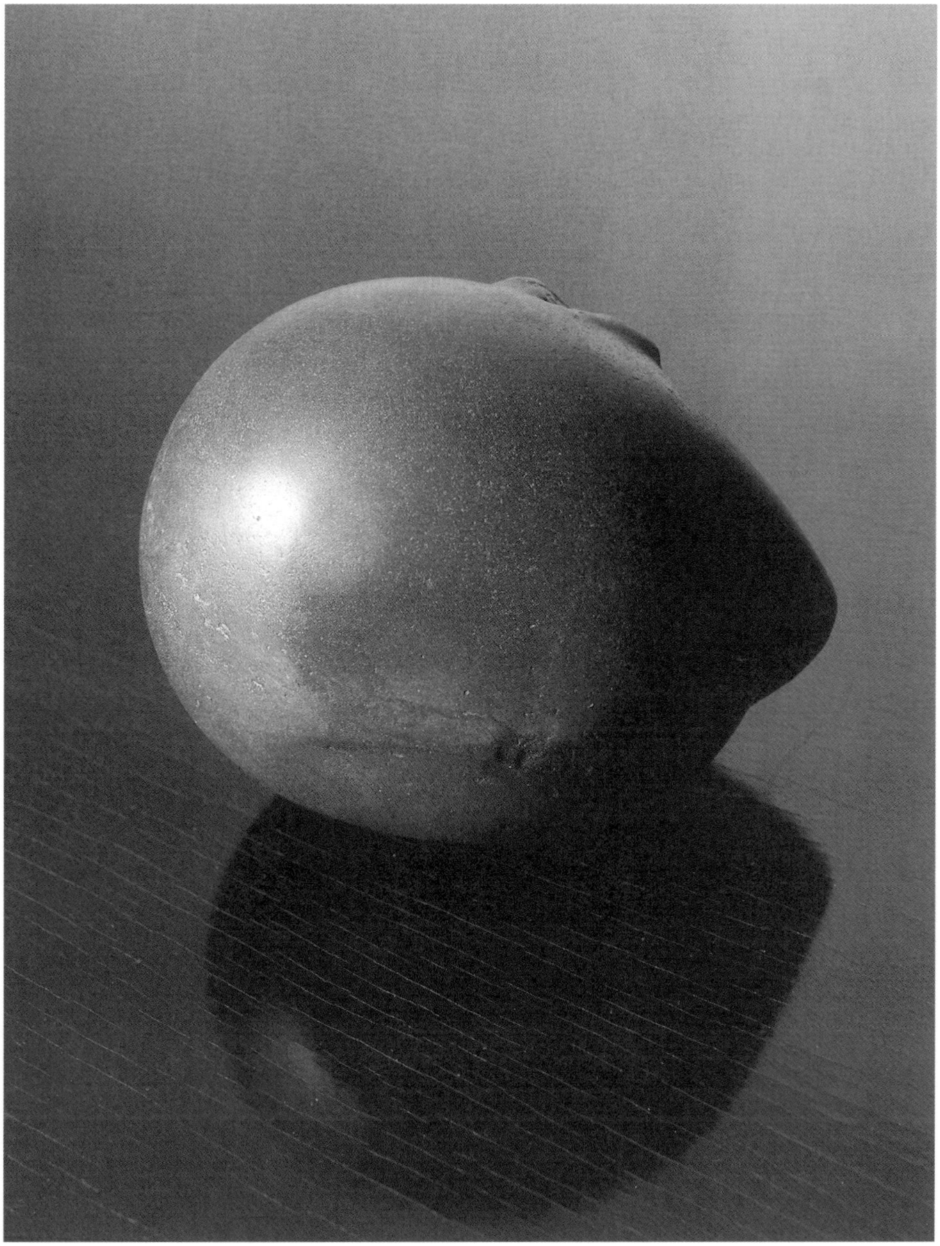

Constantin Brancusi
Prométhée (Prometheus)
c. 1912 Cat. No. 8

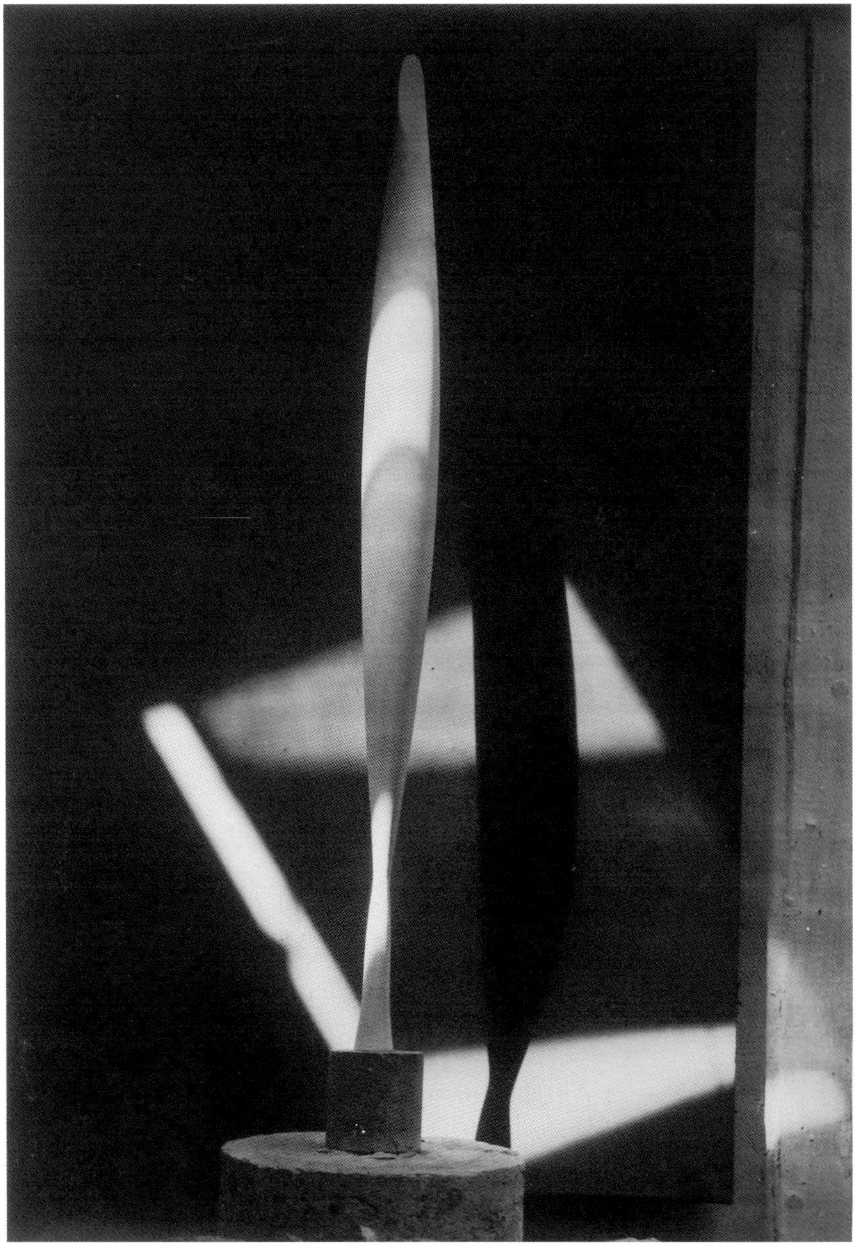

Constantin Brancusi
L'Oiseau dans l'espace (Bird in Space)
1930 Cat. No. 22

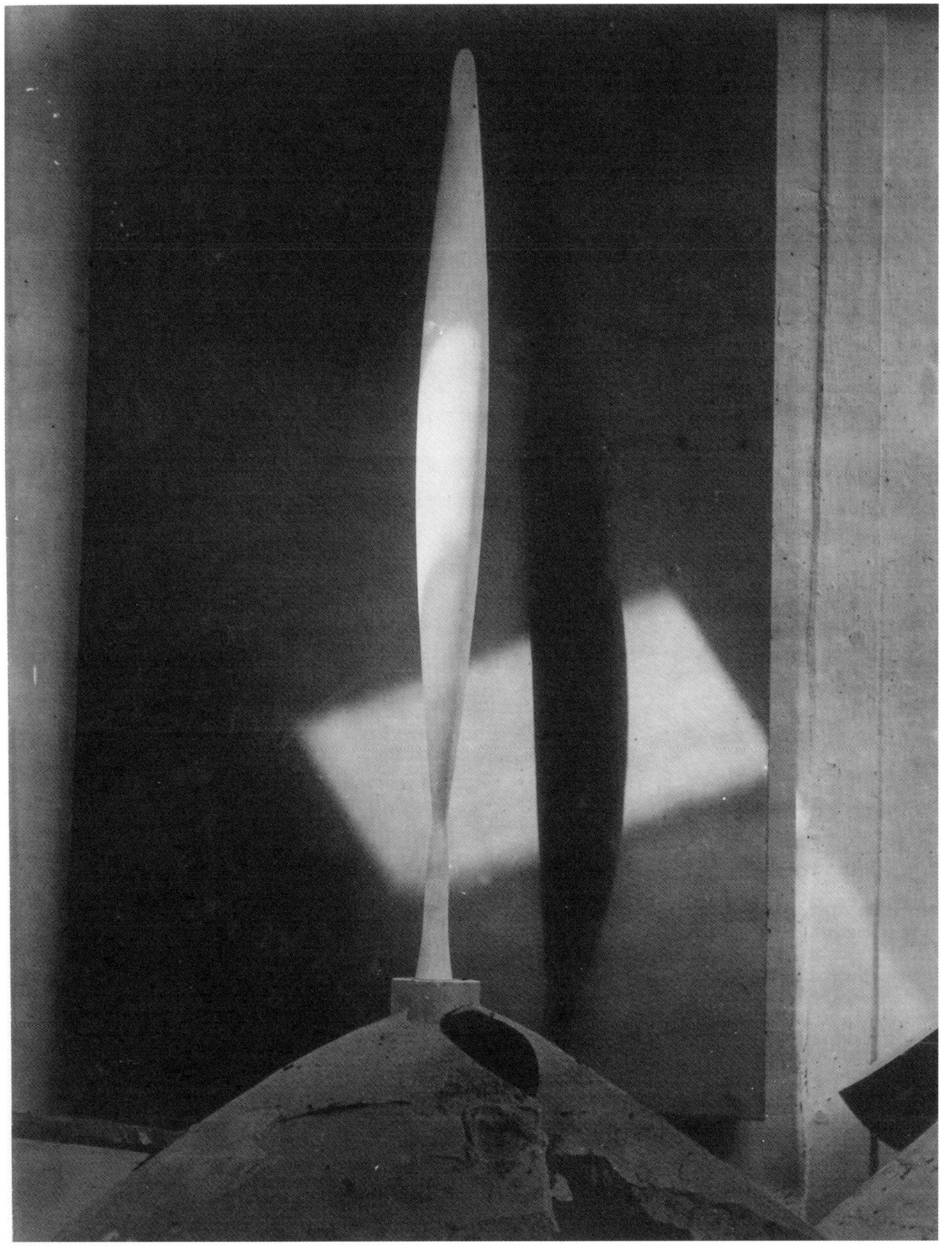

Constantin Brancusi
L'Oiseau dans l'espace (Bird in Space)
1930 Cat. No. 21

not interested in chance. The Romanian was extremely fastidious about the display of his works, which he planned down to the smallest detail, to ensure what he considered optimum viewing conditions.[22] The need to control presentation is likely to have prompted Brancusi's interest in photography. Although his works were immortalised by some of the most important photographers of his time (Edward Steichen and Alfred Stieglitz among them), Brancusi was famously dissatisfied with the results, to the extent that in the early 1920s he began to take and process his own photographs. This finally allowed him to show the sculptures in the setting and light conditions which he thought ideal, and to record the desired auratic effects and dissolution of the surface in strong light (as exemplified by the series of images of **Mlle. Pogany II**, 1920; cat. nos. 13-15). From this point of view, photography provided Brancusi with a useful tool to record alternative ways of looking at sculpture, as it had done for Rodin. The immediacy and easy repeatability of the medium, however, also allowed the artist a greater degree of control over time, the dimension that was most difficult to govern in the sculptures. This was clearly crucial for Brancusi, as is demonstrated by his interest in producing sequences of photographs in which a sculpture is seen under changing natural or artificial light over a period of time (one of the most remarkable of these is the series of six photographs of **Bird in Space** taken in 1930, two of which are in the exhibition; cat. nos. 21 and 22). Although he never treated it as art to be displayed, photography somehow represented the culmination of Brancusi's quest for formal perfection, in that, Platonically, when 'frozen' in a photographic image sculpture appears one step further removed from the accidents of nature and one step closer to the 'essence of things'.

Although in 1914 he made a version of **Sleeping Muse II** in translucent alabaster, Brancusi did not show a great interest in transparency. This was of much more importance to Gabo and Moholy-Nagy. The Russian regarded transparency as a crucial device to pursue his investigation into a sculpture made of real space. It is thanks to light showing through translucent materials such as glass and plastics that it is possible to convey a sense of volume (as opposed to solid mass) and

22. Of *Prometheus*, for instance, Brancusi said that only "if it is properly set you see how it falls on his shoulder as the eagle devoured his liver." (in D. Lewis, *Brancusi*, London 1957, p. 37). Towards the end of his life, this became almost an obsession, to the point that Brancusi was reluctant to remove any of the sculptures from the studio in fear of spoiling the arrangement of the whole. And when the time came to donate his studio with its contents to the French state, he did so on the condition that it should be kept together and retain the display he had designed.

dynamism. Gabo was not interested in transparency for its aesthetic appeal or ideological value. His choice of Plexiglas and other industrial products was not dictated by a wish to celebrate modernity but, rather, by his adherence to the Modernist sculptural principle of 'truth to materials'.[23]

Reflection played a lesser role in Gabo's aesthetic than in Brancusi's. An example of its investigation in his work is offered by **Linear Construction No.2** (cat. no. 29), in which the use of nylon filament creates an ambiguous interplay between solid and void which is enhanced by the reflectivity of the thread and the colourless shadows it creates. In Gabo's work light itself did not become the object of a systematic investigation, remaining somehow a useful tool to achieve the desired spatial effects, or occasionally to investigate sculptural ideas, as in the case of the photographs of light pattern he took and retouched in 1941 (cat. nos. 37 a-e). But, with the exception of a project for a light festival in Berlin (1928) and, in part, the designs for Diaghilev's ballet *La Chatte* (1927), Gabo never explored the direct and controlled use of light. This, instead, became the primary focus in Moholy-Nagy's work. The Hungarian coined for himself the term *Lichtner* (manipulator of light) and promoted the idea of an 'Academy of Light'.[24] Moholy's entire career, in fact, revolved around the ideal of an art of light, which he pursued in painting, sculpture, photography, film, design, and as a writer, editor and teacher.

Moholy's interest in the study of light emerged in the first half of the 1920s, when he created the series of 'glass architecture' pictures. Paul Scheerbart's and Adolf Behne's theories of glass architecture were very influential on Moholy in his early years. He tried to translate their ideas into two-dimensional works in different techniques, like the lithograph **Gradations** (1924; cat. no. 40) or the woodcuts and linocuts that he published in the magazine *Der Sturm* from 1922 (see the two **Compositions** and **Variation**; cat. nos. 38, 39 and 41). These works are characterised by compositions with a defined architectural character, in which the interplay of planes and light is ambiguous and animated by the suggestion of transparency, and with complex relationships between foreground and background, often with almost *trompe-l'oeil* effects.

23. "My materials are not chosen for their aesthetic appeal – for their texture or colour – but to give more freedom to the space. Transparency was the obvious answer and so I used glass." (N. Gabo interviewed by Rackstraw Downes, "Listening to Gabo" in *Granta*, Cambridge, vol. LXVI, no. 1281, 19 May 1962, p. 7).
24. See L. Moholy-Nagy, "Light Painting", in J.L. Martin, B. Nicholson and N. Gabo, *op. cit.*, pp. 245-7.

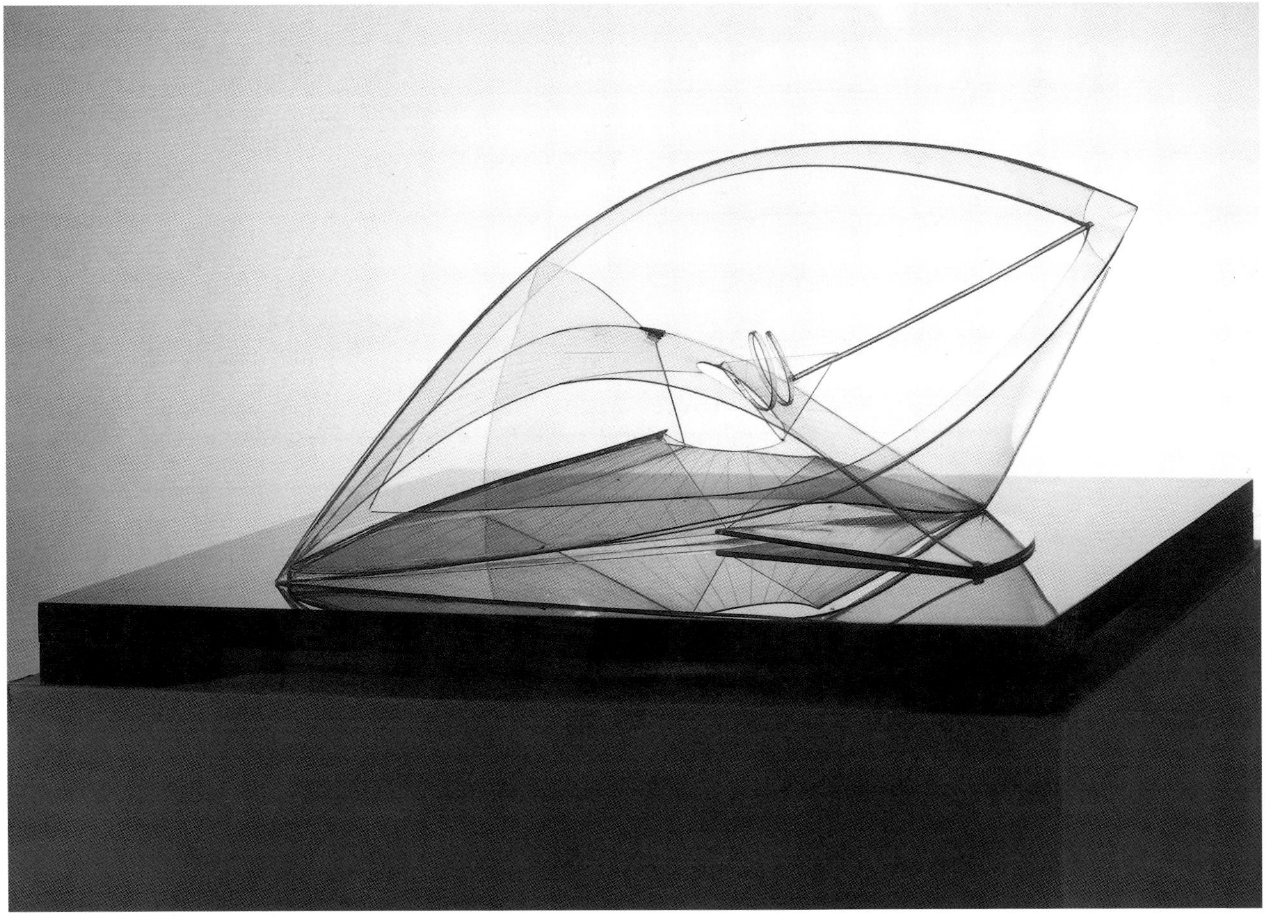

Naum Gabo
Spiral Theme
1941 Cat. No. 28

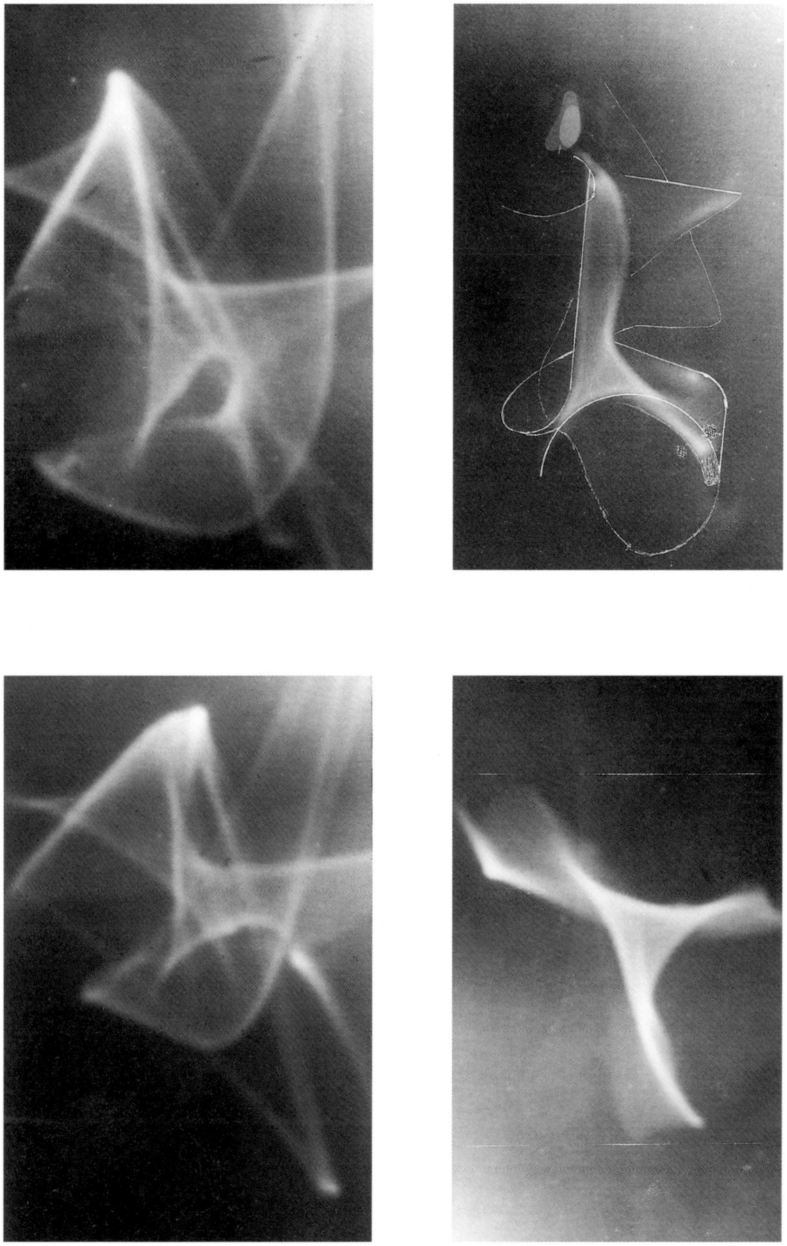

Naum Gabo
photographs of reflected light pattern
1941 Cat. No. 37

It was in paintings like **G 8** (1926; cat. no. 42), however, that Moholy truly challenged the relationship between two- and three-dimensional space. Painted on both sides of a sheet of Galalith (a type of celluloid), which is separated by a few millimetres from the cardboard background, the work is constructed around the complicated interplay of real planes showing through one another. The compositional structure becomes aligned with the diagonal of the support, and is thus freed from gravity, becoming lighter and airier. The theme of the floating diagonal cross (a clear homage to Suprematism) echoes the earlier prints, but here the floating form is repeated in different positions and sizes, increasing the sense of suspension and dynamism.

Despite the rich output and experimentation with various materials (including aluminium), Moholy was not completely satisfied with the light effects he could achieve in painting and printmaking and transferred his attention to photography. Here he began to experiment with the direct use of real light, which soon became his preferred medium. In particular, his camera-less photographs (which he called 'photograms'[25]) rapidly acquired so much artistic relevance that Moholy recognised in them the potential to take over the role of painting.

The photogram was, for Moholy, the highest form of static light composition, and it allowed him to replace pigment with real light, an aspiration which the artist theorised in numerous of his writings.[26] What is interesting, in terms of dematerialising effects, is the fact that the photogram, a negative image, reverses the conventional relationship between light and dark. This makes solid bodies look light and weightless in a space that has become dark and very physical. The photogram was therefore a prime example of what Moholy-Nagy intended for a new language of

25. The photogram technique pre-dates the invention of camera photography. It is thought to have been invented by William Henry Fox Talbot in the early 1830s. A photogram is obtained by placing objects on light-sensitive paper and exposing them to light for variable lengths of time. The Dadaists, Christian Schad and Man Ray, began to explore the expressive potential of the technique from c.1919. Moholy thus described his use of it: "light is allowed to fall on to a screen (photographic plate, light-sensitive paper) through objects with different coefficients of refraction or to be deflected from its original path by various contrivances; certain parts of the screen are shaded, etc. This process can occur with or without camera (in the second case the technique of the process consists in fixing a differentiated play of light and shadow)." (from *Malerei, Fotografie, Film*, cit., p. 32). Occasionally, a 'positive' white-background version could be created by shining a strong light through the original photogram and a sheet of light-sensitive paper placed over it. On Moholy's photography, see Geraldine A. Johnson's essay.
26. See, for example, Moholy's *From Pigment to Light*, published in 1933 (reproduced in K. Passuth, *Moholy-Nagy*, London 1985, pp. 323-326).

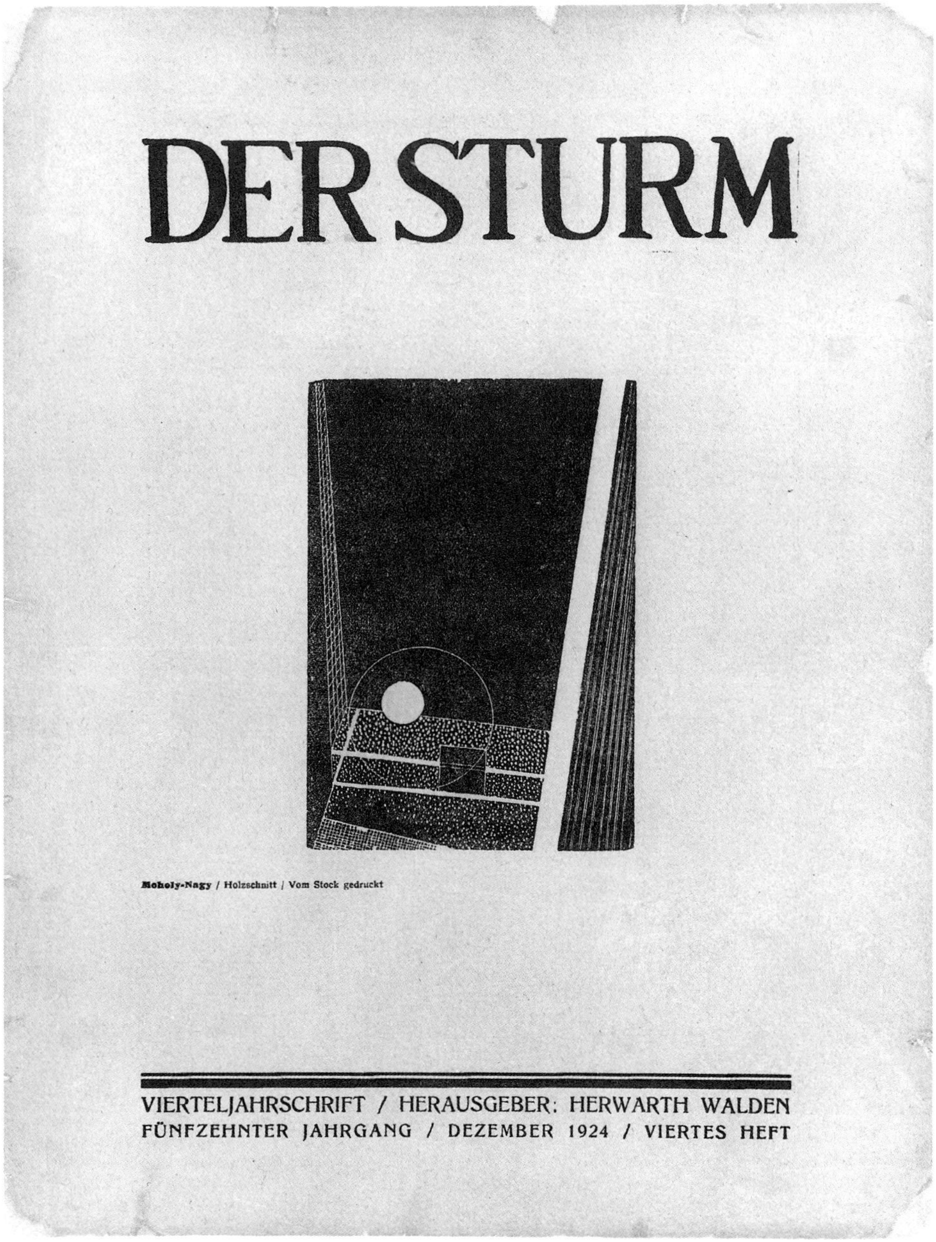

DER STURM

Moholy-Nagy / Holzschnitt / Vom Stock gedruckt

VIERTELJAHRSCHRIFT / HERAUSGEBER: HERWARTH WALDEN
FÜNFZEHNTER JAHRGANG / DEZEMBER 1924 / VIERTES HEFT

László Moholy-Nagy
Variation
1924 Cat. No. 39

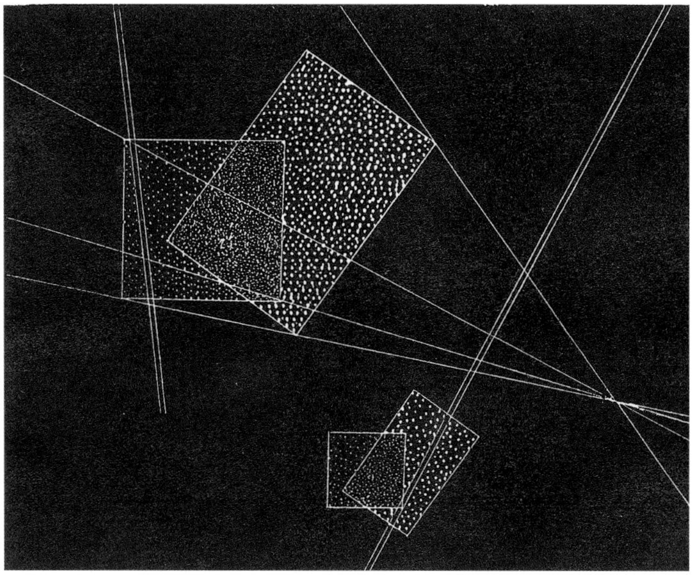

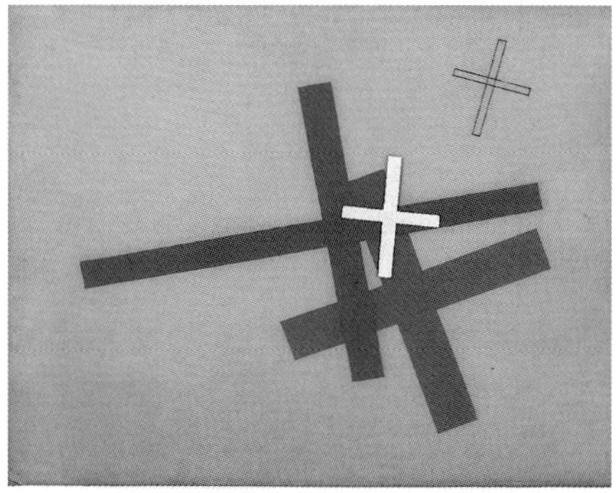

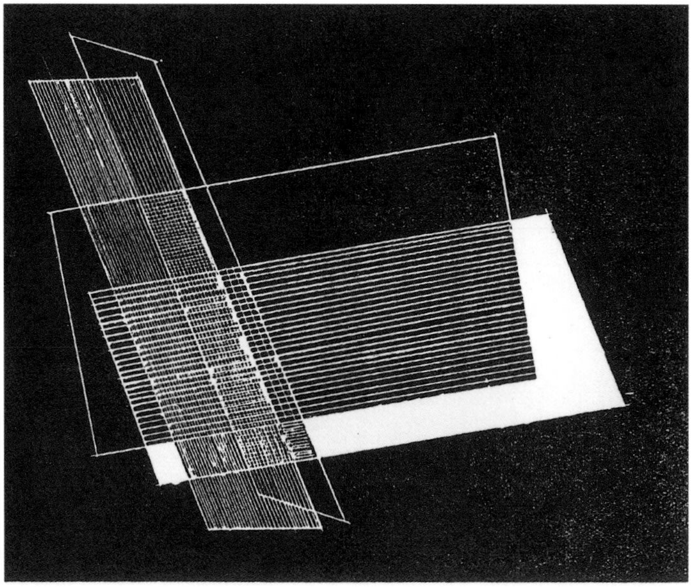

László Moholy-Nagy

Komposition (Composition)
c. 1923 Cat. No. 38

Komposition (Composition)
1925 Cat. No. 41

G 8 (three-dimensional painting)
c. 1926 Cat. No. 42

Untitled photogram
1925-28 Cat. No. 54

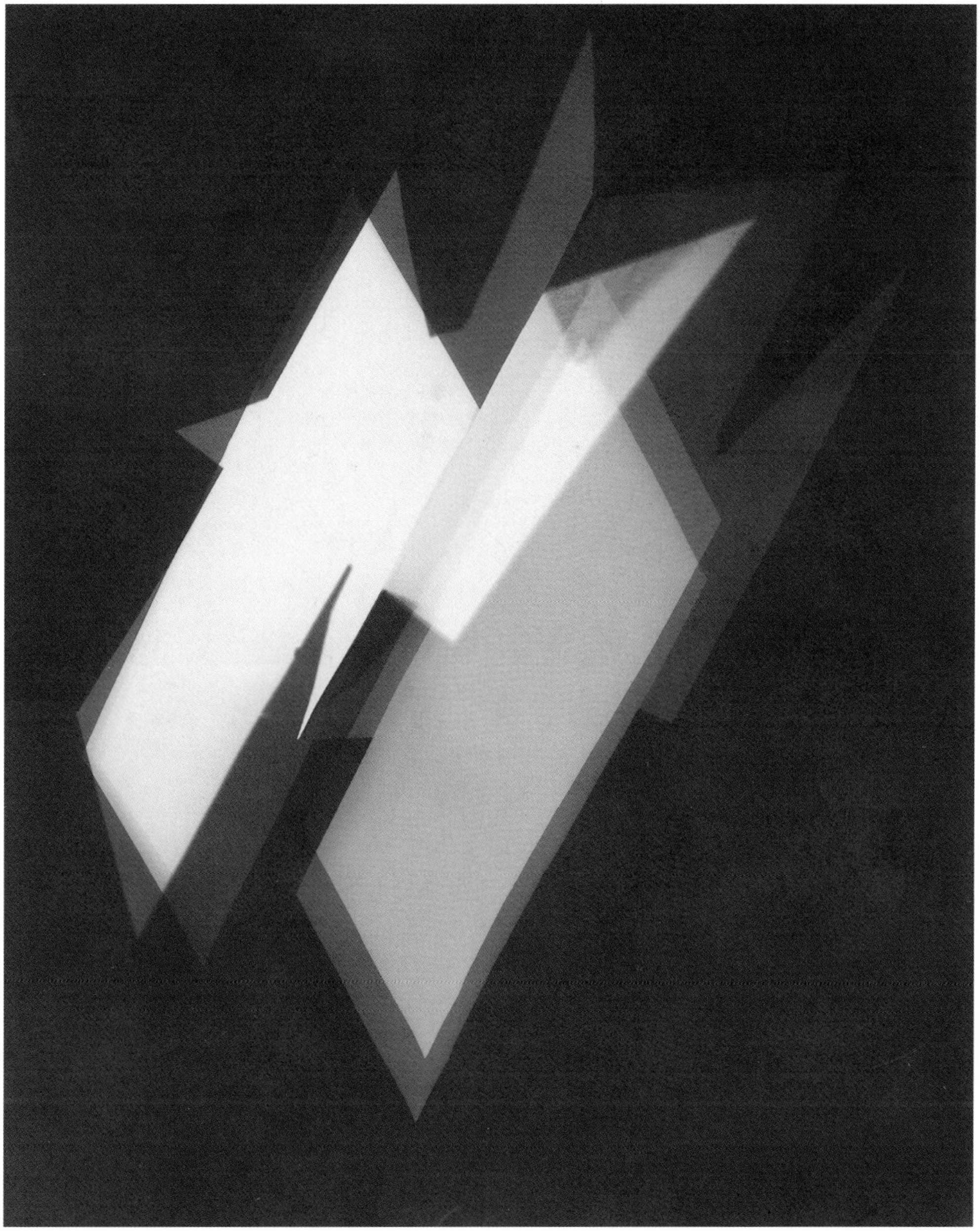

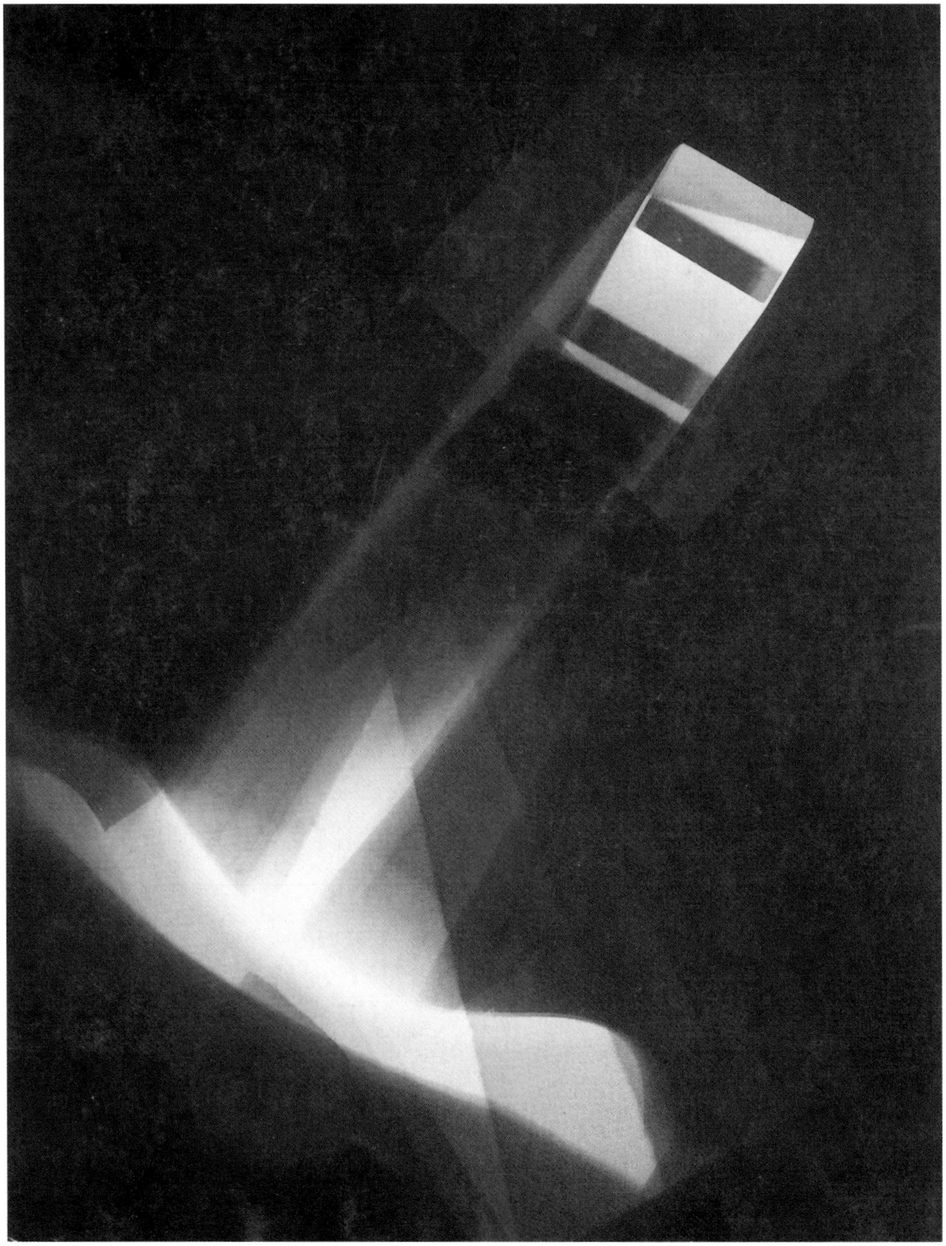

László Moholy-Nagy
Untitled photogram
1925-28 Cat. No. 48

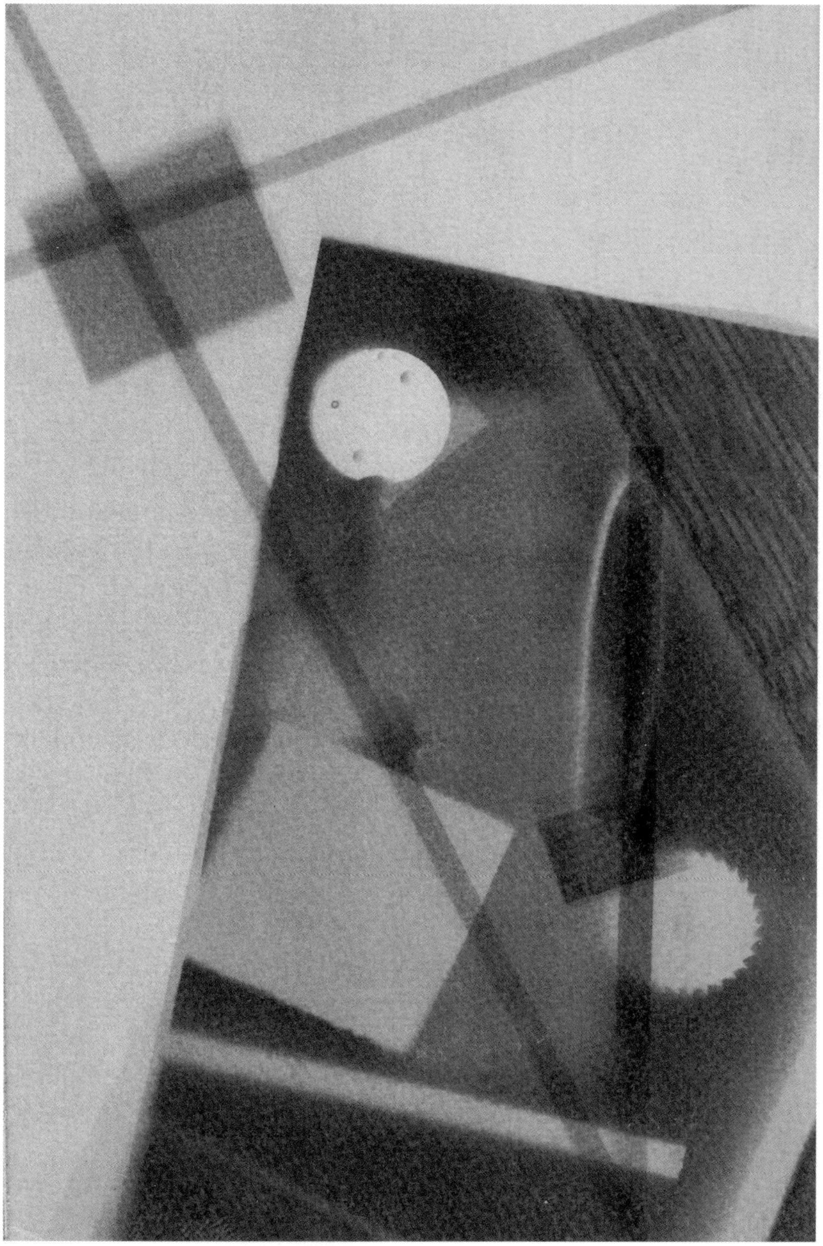

László Moholy-Nagy
Untitled photogram
1922 Cat. No. 44

light, space and time. Throughout his career the artist explored the technique in hundreds of variants, producing immaterial images with very subtle tonal variations, which also exploit the brown and green nuances of the paper itself.

The photogram, with its distinctly three-dimensional feel, allowed Moholy-Nagy to conduct his research on the boundary between sculpture and photography. The artist actually made constructed pieces from the early 1920s, when he created works in wood and metal. This strand of his art was temporarily put aside during the years he spent at the Bauhaus (1922-28), where sculpture was regarded with some scepticism because of its minimal practical value, and while living in London, where the pressures to make a living forced him to concentrate on design and teaching. After moving to the US, however, in the late 1930s Moholy resumed his interest in sculpture, creating a number of suspended and cantilevered Plexiglas pieces. Transparent, highly workable and pliable, Plexiglas allowed Moholy, who was partly inspired in this by Gabo's work, to use translucent planes which could be perforated, made concave or convex and, with the use of light sources such as spotlights or moving lamps, create fascinating visual effects. **Leda and the Swan** and **Spirals** (both from 1946, the year of the artist's death; cat. nos. 57 and 58) are two mesmerising examples of Moholy-Nagy's late three-dimensional pieces, which, as he specified, were not sculptures but 'space-modulators'.

Gabo's early experiments had also been crucial to the development of what is probably Moholy's masterpiece, the **Light-Space Modulator** (1922-30). Gabo had been the first to investigate the introduction of real movement in sculpture, in c.1919-20, when he had made the experimental **Kinetic Construction (Standing Wave)** (cat. no. 25). Like Moholy-Nagy, Gabo regarded movement as the most effective way of introducing real time into sculpture, a concern which was at the foundation of Constructivist art. Until Gabo's experiments with real motion, sculptors had only attempted to represent movement through illusionism or suggestion. With a seminal shift in perspective, the Russian theorised that time could only become an element of art if real movement of substantial masses was involved. His efforts in this direction, however, were frustrated by the impossibility of creating the kinetic schemes he aspired to without obtrusive and very physical mechanisms, and so **Kinetic Construction** remained an experiment. His dissatisfaction with the limitations imposed by technology later led Gabo to investigate the possibility of reversing the dynamic relationship between sculpture and viewer, utilising, for example, the movement of the latter. This is the principle behind **Construction Suspended in Space** (1956, Baltimore), conceived to be displayed at the centre of a spiral staircase from which it is seen while walking up and down and around it.[27] In search of alternative ways of combining his revolutionary approach to three-dimensional volume with movement, Gabo also turned to theatre. In 1927 he designed sets and costumes in transparent materials for Diaghilev's ballet *La Chatte*, which he conceived as a spectacle of synchronised movements of dancers, light and music. The following year he also made a project for a film in which the dynamic principles developed for the ballet would be applied to his sculptures, which would be filmed in motion to various musical soundtracks.[28]

Moholy was well aware of Gabo's experimentation with motion, and he also stimulated similar research at the Bauhaus.[29] The Hungarian theorised a natural evolution in art which would lead to what he defined as 'equipoised sculpture' (made in glass or other translucent materials and suspended using thin transparent wires, magnetic forces or electric remote control). 'Kinetic equipoise' would go even further: in it volume relationships would be virtual, "resulting mainly from the actual movement of the contours, rings, rods, and other objects. Here the material is employed as a vehicle of motion. To the three dimensions of volume, a fourth – movement – (in other words *time*) is added."[30] Light would obviously play a key role in this new sculpture: "Light – as a time-spatial energy and its projection – is an outstanding aid in propelling kinetic sculpture, and in attaining virtual volume."[31]

The **Light-Space Modulator** represented the culmination of this research. It is a mechanical apparatus made from a rotating disc with three metal frames whose edges meet, a glass spiral, three metal screens and two perforated metal discs. All the metal parts are brightly polished and the light that the machine projects is both reflected and modulated by these, creating ever-changing effects of light and

27. The idea of kinetic sculpture, however, remained at the forefront of Gabo's mind. In 1957-58, for instance, he made a motorised sculpture, the revolving *Linear Construction in Space No.4*.
28. This project, which never came to life, is described in a letter to Dr Guido Bagier, 14 October 1928 (published in M. Hammer and C. Lodder, *op. cit.*, pp. 49-51).
29. Experiments on movement in sculpture were conducted in the Plastic Workshop. In 1928, for instance, Edmund Collein and Heinz Loew created a series of light-sculpture studies consisting of a fast revolving plate with a rod mounted diagonally, which at speed and with the right lighting created virtual volumes.
30. L. Moholy-Nagy, *The New Vision*, cit., p. 47.
31. *Ibid.*, p. 50.

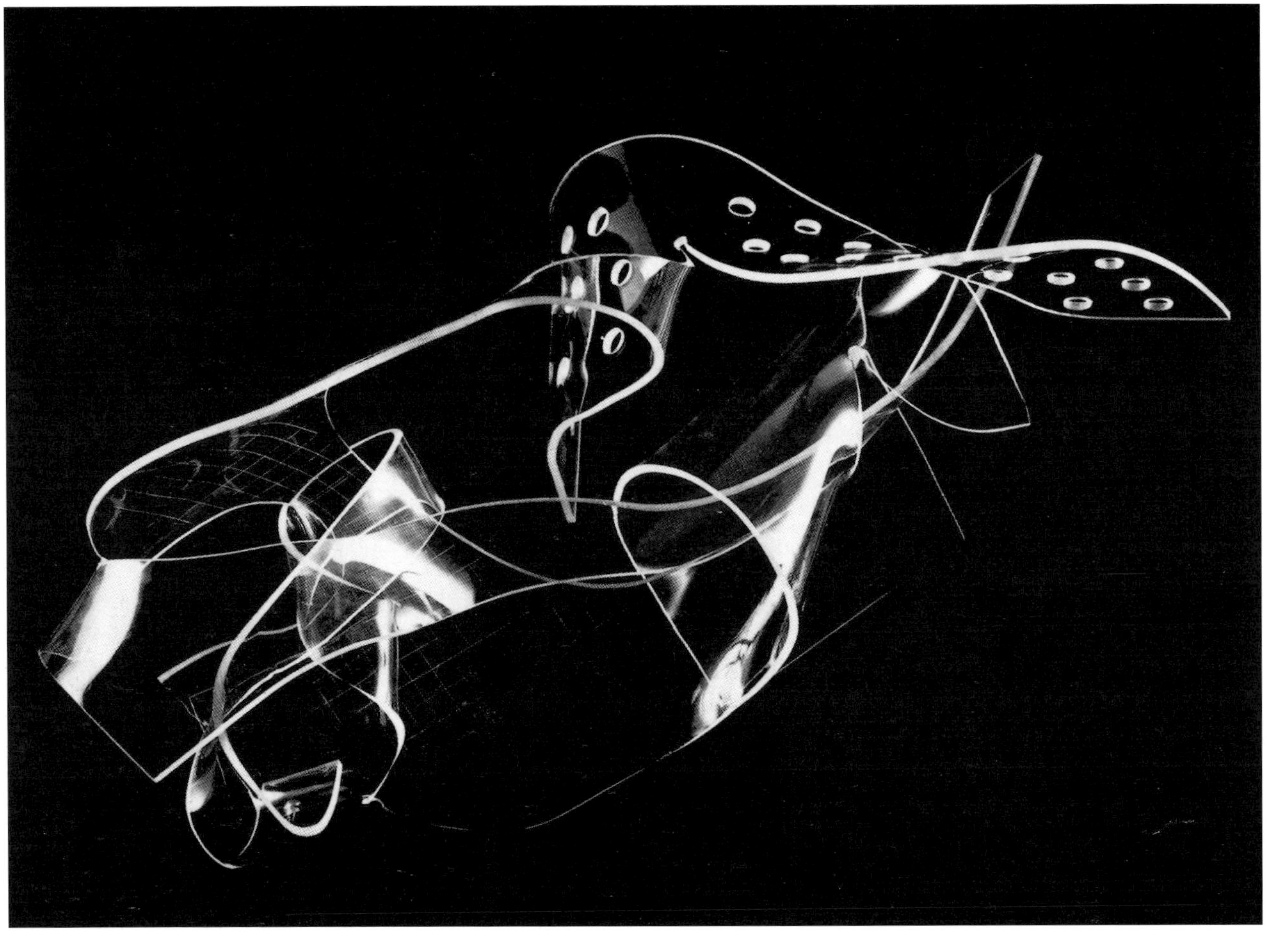

László Moholy-Nagy
Spirals
1946 (replica 1977) Cat. No. 58

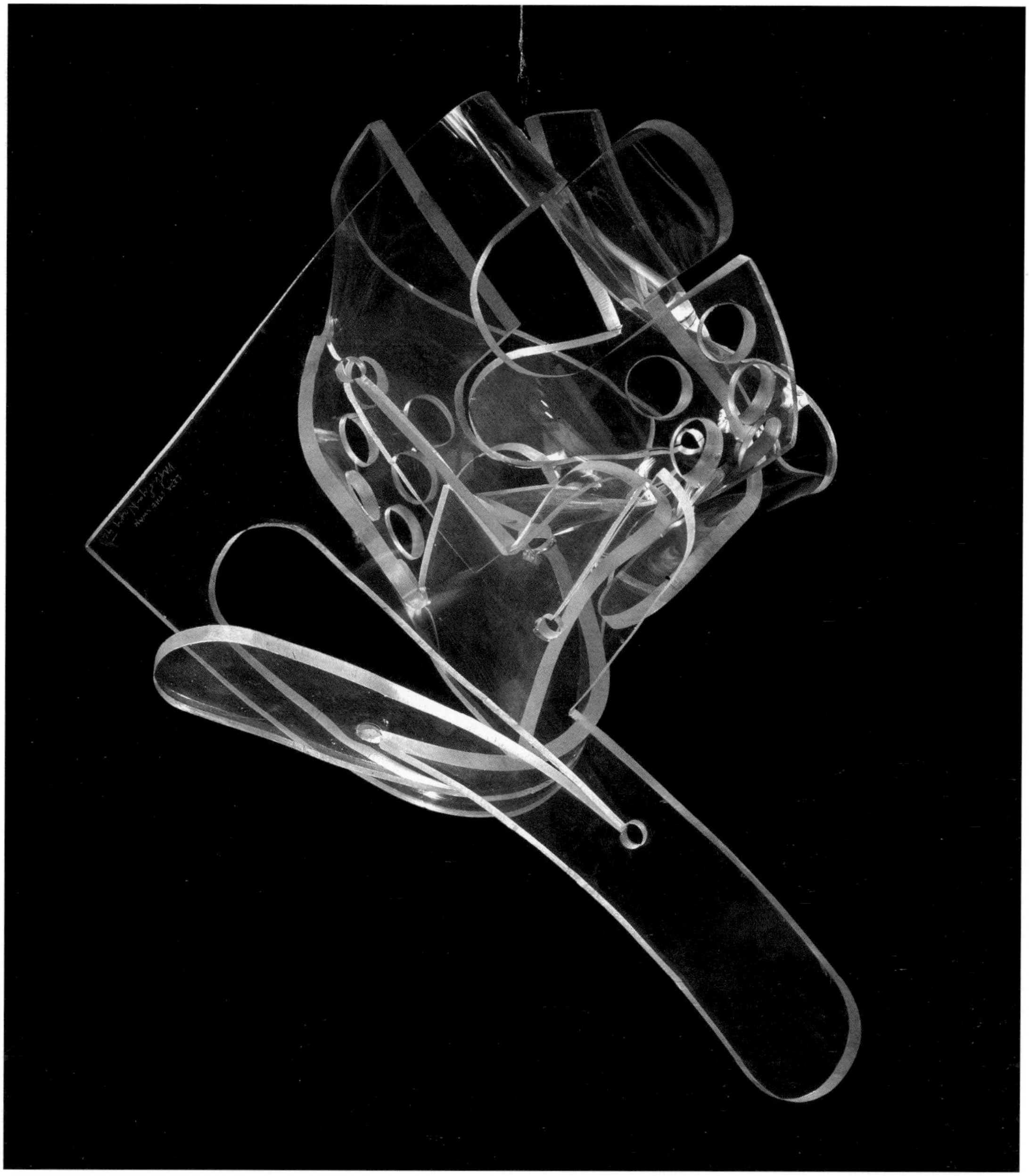

László Moholy-Nagy
Leda and the Swan
1946 Cat. No. 57

shadow. The truly revolutionary aspect of the **Light-Space Modulator** is that it only exists as the combination of the actual machine and as its immaterial light-show. In other words, it only exists in movement, and that makes it the first 'sculpture' truly to defy the stasis and weightiness of traditional plastic art. Moholy also worked on projects for light displays both outdoors (using neon and searchlights, sky-writers and projections onto clouds) and indoors (reflected light displays; the 'color-piano' with a keyboard connected with graduated lamps; and 'light-fresco' to animate architecture). And, like Gabo, he was interested in theatre, and wrote extensively on it.[32]

The use of movement in sculpture to create effects of dematerialisation also concerned Brancusi. The artist saw the **Light-Space Modulator** when it was shown for the first time in Paris, at the 1930 Exposition des Arts Décoratifs. The mesmerising dynamics and light play of the piece had a major impact on those who saw it, and it is possible that it was this that inspired Brancusi to display his **Leda** (cat. no. 10) on a slowly revolving motorised base. This arrangement allowed the sculpture to reflect light from different positions and at varying intensity during the day, conveying a sense of perpetual metamorphosis which is, in fact, the theme of the work.[33] It is only when seen in motion that the sculpture really becomes Leda, an ever-changing figure which is, in Brancusi's words, "endlessly creating a new life, a new rhythm."[34]

Brancusi was very subtle in his treatment of movement, and he was often able to include it in his work only as an allusion. This is evident in a piece like the **Endless Column**, which is intended to evoke the flight of a bird by showing it in a sequence of ascending positions, with a concept similar to the succession of images in chronophotography. The idea of seriality is not of secondary importance in Brancusi's work.[35] The artist frequently produced series of sculptures, like those of

32. See the 1922 Bauhaus book *Die Bühne im Bauhaus* (The Theatre in the Bauhaus). Interestingly, Moholy regarded theatre as a purely visual experience, in which actors could be replaced by mechanical puppets and light play was central (he suggested the use of beams of coloured light emanating from reflectors and filtered by screens).
33. The work is based on the myth of Leda and the swan, although, interestingly, for Brancusi it is not Zeus but Leda herself who becomes a swan.
34. Quoted in F.T. Bach, *Brancusi 1876-1957*, Paris 1995, p. 19 (my translation). Here the artist is clearly echoing Bergson's concept of the real as a continuously changing entity.
35. Brancusi was an important inspiration for many Minimalists, in particular Carl Andre and Robert Morris. On this, see Sylvie Coëllier, "Brancusi/Carl Andre: Une question d'espace", in *Cahiers du Musée national d'art modern*, no. 47, spring 1994.

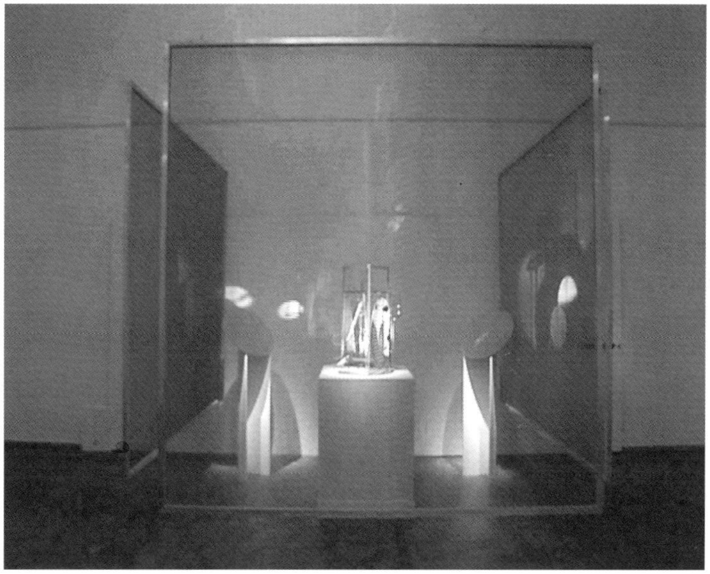

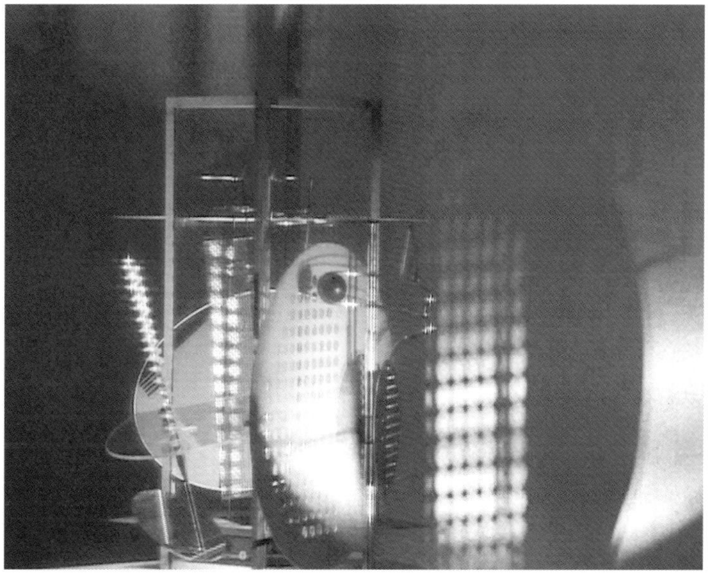

László Moholy-Nagy
Light-Space Modulator
1922-30
(stills from film of installation at
Bauhaus-Archiv, Berlin)

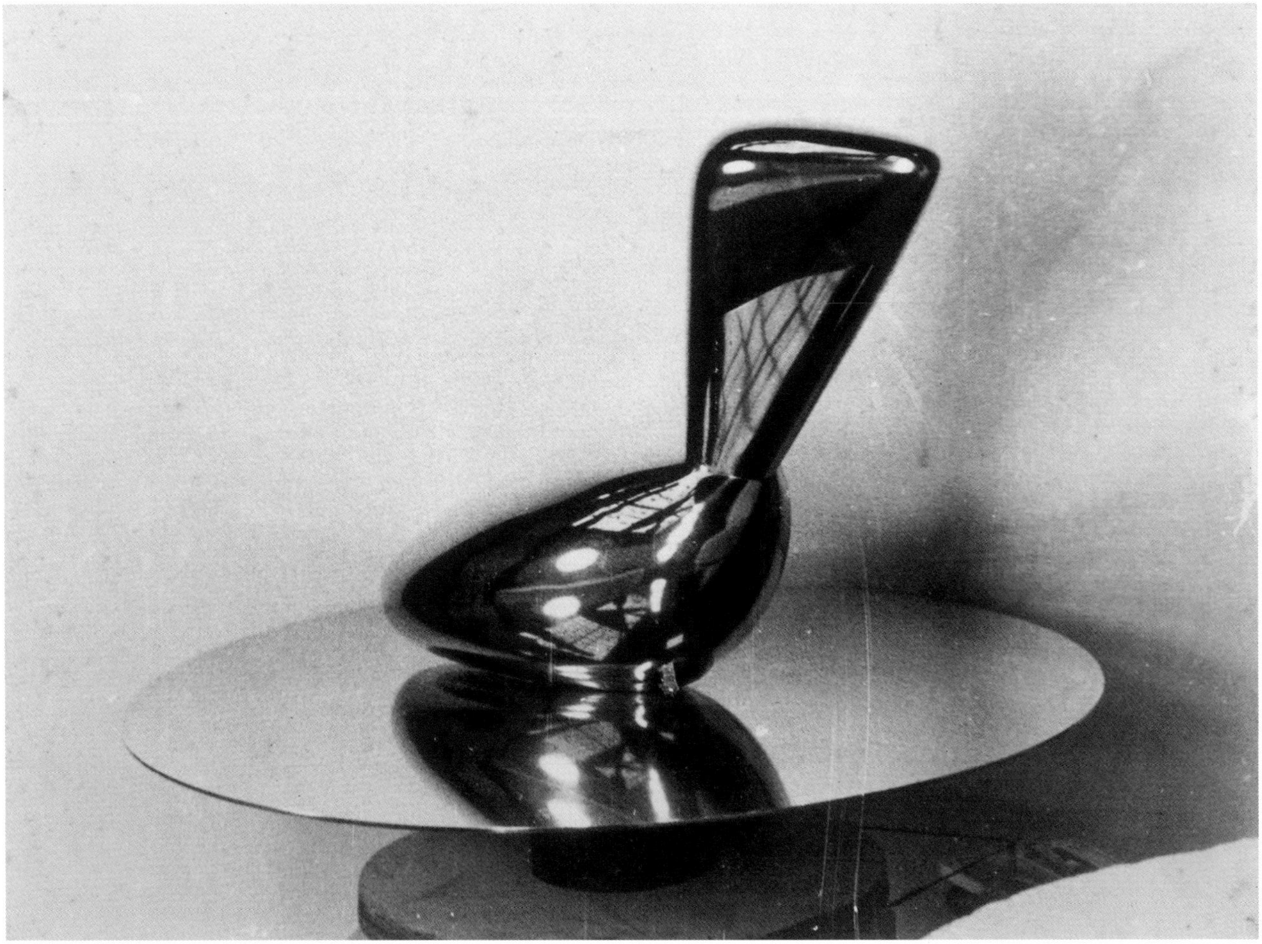

Constantin Brancusi
Leda
1925-26 Cat. No. 16

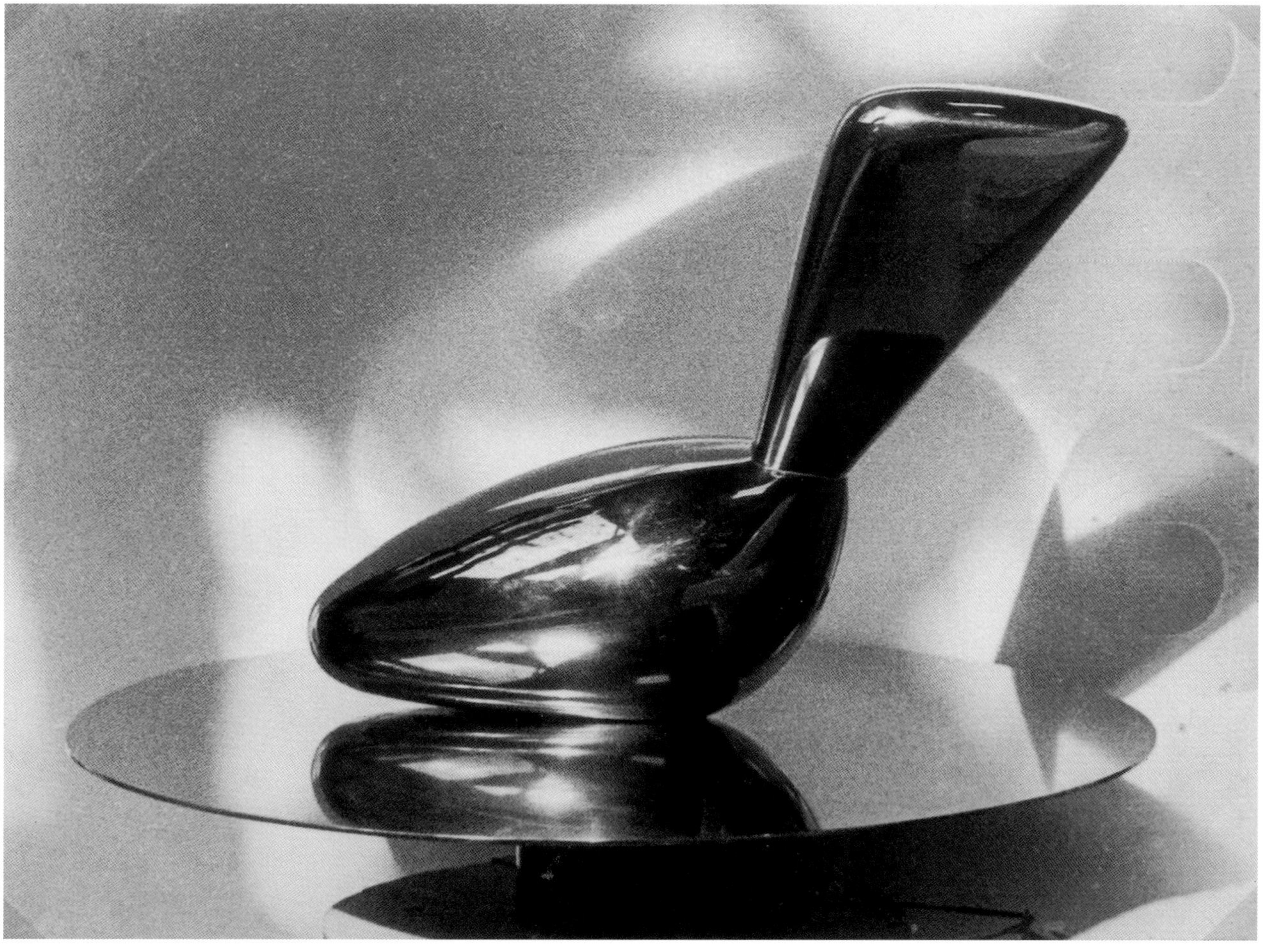

Constantin Brancusi
Leda
1925-26 Cat. No. 17

birds, in which a progressive formal refinement and simplification corresponds to an increasing elongation of the figure (for an example, see the development of **Cock** – cat. no. 9). It seems, somehow, that it is the sequence of works, rather then the individual pieces, that succeeds in conveying the sense of a bird's flight. In this sense, Brancusi appears to have had a nearly 'cinematic' approach, as the formal development within each series of birds almost recalls a sequence of photograms in a film. The sculptor did, in fact, make some attempts to work with film. The images of **Leda** in the exhibition (cat. nos. 16-18), for instance, were originally frames from a 35mm film of the revolving sculpture made by Brancusi, who then re-photographed the negative film.

The moving image played a crucial role in the development of Moholy-Nagy's art of light in motion. The artist made eleven films between 1926 and 1936. While the majority of these are social documentaries on aspects of modern life in Germany, France and Britain, **Ein Lichtspiel Schwarz-Weiß-Grau** (Light Play: Black-White-Grey; cat. no. 55), made in c.1932, epitomises the artist's idea of film as the highest expression of an art combining the modern artistic materials of light and movement. The film shows the **Light-Space Modulator** in motion, emphasising its mesmerising play of light and shadow. It is, in a way, even more successful than the machine in this, because it is completely virtual, just a projection of light, without the weight of the physical materials with which the **Modulator** was built.[36]

Another strategy to create a sense of dematerialisation in sculpture is the challenge to traditional notions of equilibrium and balance. Examples of this are Gabo's **Linear Construction No.2** and Moholy's **Leda and the Swan**, which are suspended from an 'invisible' wire, or Moholy's **Spirals**, which was originally affixed to a black rectangular slab of Formica in a cantilevered position. Suspension and precarious balance are effective ways of challenging the weightiness of the sculptural object, because they nullify its traditional, earth-bound relationship with the base and, through instability, they help convey a sense of dynamism, or even introduce actual movement.

36. As with everything else, Moholy-Nagy had a very experimental attitude to cinema: he made projects for showing different films simultaneously to form a dynamic whole; and he also thought of fitting a rotating prism in front of the lens of the projector, or of having a spherical screen. For Moholy the physically pure light projections offered much more than hand-made painting ever could.

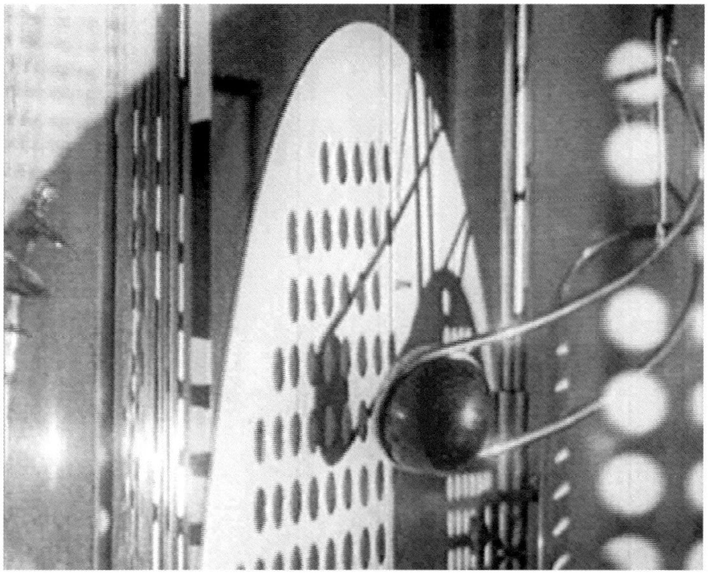

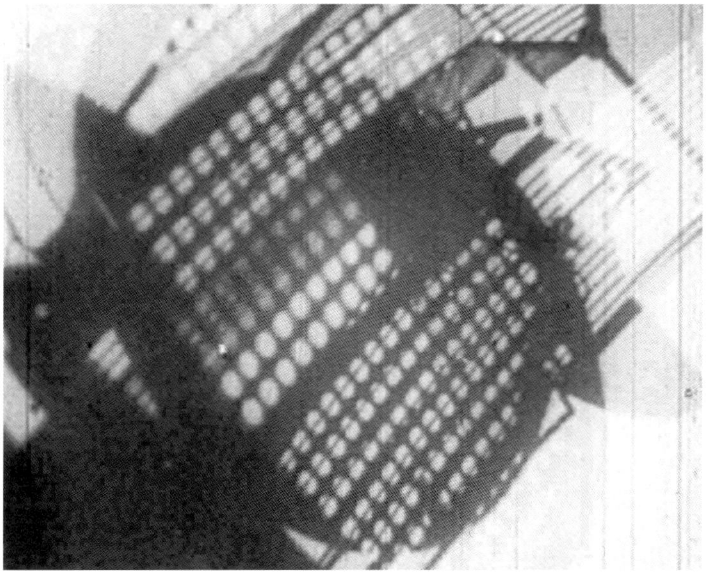

László Moholy-Nagy
stills from the film
Ein Lichtspiel Schwarz-Weiß-Grau
(Light Play Black-White-Grey)
1932 Cat. No. 55

The separation of sculpture from the base was one of Brancusi's key innovations. The Romanian challenged the traditional inseparability of the two, and made bases to display his sculptures which were visually very obviously different from them. Many of his polished bronze pieces, like **Fish** (cat. no. 11), were placed on heavy, light-absorbing wooden bases which emphasise, by contrast, the lightness of the bright and gleaming sculptures. Similarly, Brancusi's interest in flight and vertical leap, which led him to make increasingly thinner and taller sculptures, introduced the question of their precarious balance on the base. This dovetails with another recurrent feature in the art of the Romanian, the tendency to make works with increasingly uneven distribution of the weight – with thinner bottoms and heavier tops, as exemplified by **Cock**. This was, again, a break from the traditional methods of sculpture and a strategy to create an implicit sense of instability and, therefore, dynamism, which was also often aided by the asymmetry of the composition.

Gabo investigated the notion of equilibrium in works like **Construction in Space with Balance on Two Points** (c.1924; cat no. 26), while Moholy's never realised 'equipoise sculpture', using invisible magnetic fields to control the stability of the work, could have represented the culmination of this research. Balance was an important concept for the Hungarian. In the Preliminary Course that he taught at the Bauhaus, for instance, he invited students to explore problems of design in terms of equilibrium, which he considered one of the human senses. This interest mainly derived from his belief that a full sensorial education was necessary to codify and organise the experiences which recent developments in science and industrial processes had made unpredictable.[37]

Moholy was not alone in soliciting a re-evaluation of sensory experiences in response to the crisis of perception caused by the new philosophical and scientific ideas. Filippo Marinetti's *Manifesto of Tactilism* of 1921, for instance, exalted the role of touch for its intuitive and psychological value. And Brancusi made at least one

37. Moholy encouraged his students to use touch, hearing and smell to experiment with forms and materials. "Each of the senses with which we record the position of bodies helps us to grasp space. Space is known first of all by the sense of vision. This experience of the visible relations of bodies may be checked by movement – by the alteration of one's position – and by means of touch." (L. Moholy-Nagy, *The New Vision*, cit., p. 57). Moholy had an almost synaesthetic approach, conceiving his projects as a unity of form, movement, sound, light and even smell. He was, for instance, interested in Raoul Hausmann's theory of optophonetics, published in issue 1 of *G* (1923), which discussed the relationship between perception and preconception and aspired to a unity of light and sound.

marble piece (**Sculpture for the Blind**, 1916) specifically intended to be touched but not seen.[38] In the realm of the visual arts, a concept of perception based on touch without sight allows the artist to establish a disorientating, but refreshing, new relationship with the physical world, instigating the elaboration of purely mental images and the use of memory. This could also be regarded as a strategy to create more abstract and, therefore, immaterial images. In a similar way, the three artists all expressed an interest in integrating music and sound in their art,[39] a strategy which, again, presented them with the opportunity of offering a fuller sensorial experience, more in tune with the 'wealth of optical and phonetic wonders' of the new age.

In their different ways, Brancusi, Gabo and Moholy-Nagy became pioneers of dematerialisation in three-dimensional art. The preoccupation with space, movement, time and light which informed their work was to be shared by some of the most innovative artists of the 20th century, frequently with a direct acknowledgement of their influence.[40] The light environments of Lucio Fontana, the kinetic art of the Zero Group and Yves Klein's air sculptures are only a few of the many examples which could be cited of developments directly derived from the research of the three artists. And these same concerns later inspired much more radical concepts of dematerialisation, which involved a very real formal and temporal disintegration of the work of art as a strategy to challenge its very nature as a commodity.[41] In this sense, the investigation conducted by Brancusi, Gabo and Moholy explored by this exhibition could be regarded as one of the most influential outcomes of the avant-garde years and the true expression of the modernity of their art.

38. See E. Grazioli, "La *Scultura per Ciechi* di Brancusi", in *Brancusi*, Riga no. 19, 2001, pp. 325-333. Brancusi, apparently following Duchamp's suggestion, exhibited his *Sculpture for the Blind* in a cloth sack with two hand-holes, so that people would be forced to experience it exclusively through touch.
39. Brancusi loved music, above all of Romanian folk and Gregorian choirs, of which he appreciated the formal simplicity. He played violin and was a close friend of the composer, Erik Satie, who, like him, developed an essential and simplified vocabulary (on their friendship, see H. P. Roché, "Memoires de Brancusi", in *L'Oeil*, no. 29, May 1957). Brancusi often played records on a gramophone in his studio to enhance the aesthetic experience of the sculptures. Gabo thought that music was the most absolute and abstract of the abstract arts, and admired musicians for having succeeded in creating a universal language. The projects for a film and ballet are examples of his interest in the interaction of the visual arts with sound. Moholy's fascination with noise as the symbol of mechanised modernity led him to experiment with records treated with knives and needles to produce rhythmical and distorted sounds.
40. Otto Piene's *Fire Flower Power* (1967), for example, is clearly indebted to Moholy's *Light-Space Modulator*.
41. On this, see L. Lippard, *Six Years: The Dematerialization of the Art Object from 1966 to 1972*, London 1973.

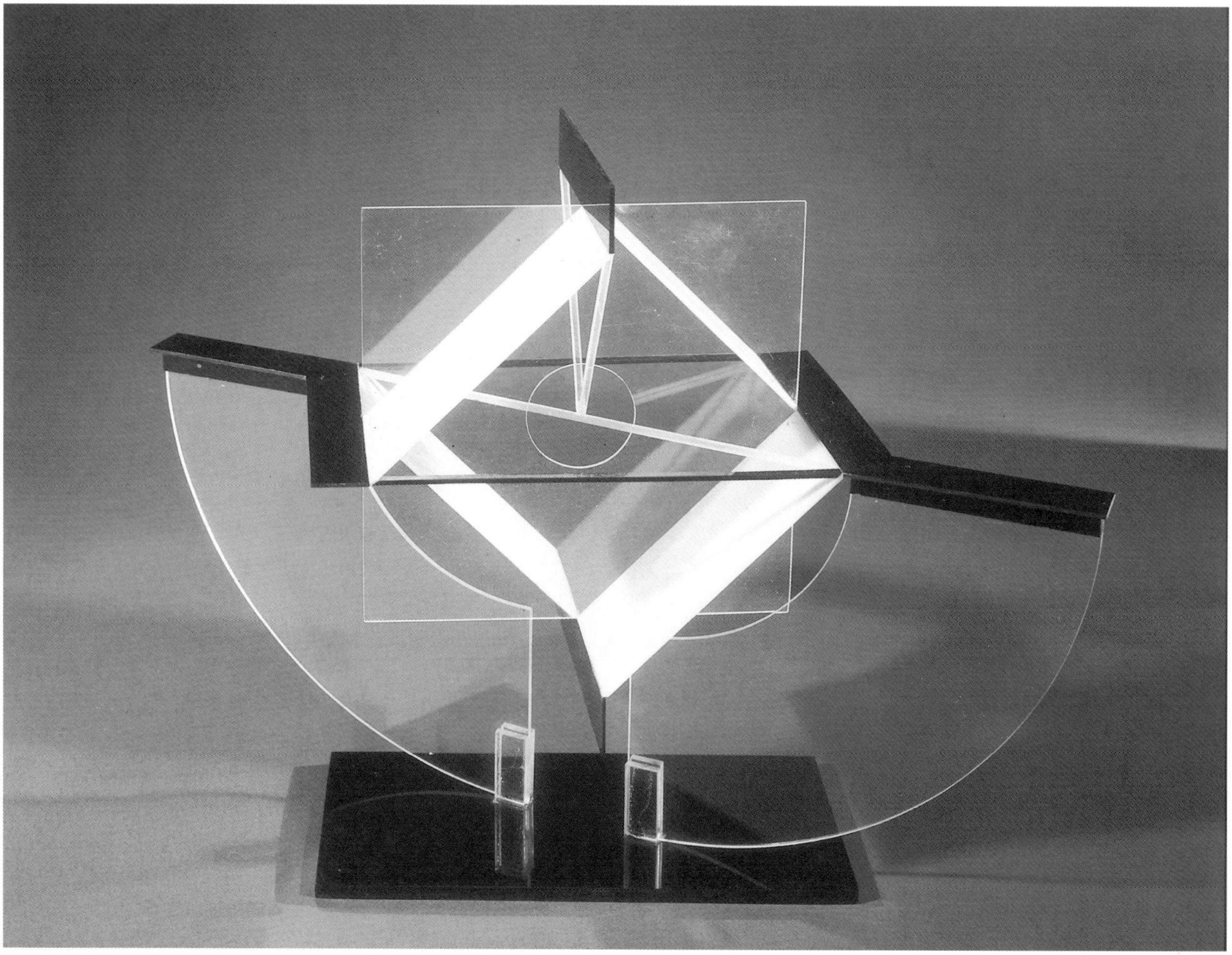

Naum Gabo
Construction in Space with Balance on Two Points
c. 1924 (assembled 1982) Cat. No. 26

DEMATERIALISING SCULPTURE: METHODS AND MOTIVES

Martin Hammer and Christina Lodder

Terms such as immaterial or, more commonly, dematerialised have been attached to a great deal of modern sculpture produced between the 1910s and the late 1960s, a period that is all too often, but none too helpfully, characterised as 'Modernism', implying that some monolithic set of attitudes prevailed. Inevitably, 'immaterial' suggests the opposite of conventional sculptural attributes like mass, solidity, monumentality, permanence, and emphatic material presence. Yet a positive definition remains elusive. As early as 1928 Moholy-Nagy's Bauhaus book *The New Vision* confidently announced that sculpture is the path "from material volume to virtual volume, and from tactile-grasp to visual-grasp", the path "to the freeing of a material from its weight: from mass to motion".[1] With hindsight, dematerialisation registers a complex array of formal and technical strategies that artists employed at this time in order to give their work a more insubstantial quality:

● One means to achieve the desired effect was to polish the surface of a solid form, so deflecting the viewer's attention away from the material realities of the work. The unusually shiny, reflective quality of many of Constantin Brancusi's cast bronze sculptures was widely emulated, as demonstrated by the recent exhibition *Shine: Sculpture and Surface in the 1920s and 1930s*.[2] The use of polished aluminium in the 1960s sculpture of David Smith and George Rickey represents a variation on this theme.

● Related approaches include the applying of a patina, varnish, or, most effectively in this context, paint. This technique is encountered in, for instance, Vladimir

1. L. Moholy-Nagy, *The New Vision*, New York 1947, p. 47 (first published 1928).
2. *Shine: Sculpture and Surface in the 1920s and 1930s*, Leeds, Henry Moore Institute, Essays on Sculpture, No. 36, 2002.

Tatlin's **Model for a Monument to the Third International** of 1920, and Aleksandr Rodchenko's hanging constructions shown in Moscow the following spring, both of which were made of wood, painted silver to look like modern steel. Paint was also used in Katarzyna Kobro's polychrome, quasi-architectural constructions from the 1920s, in many of Alexander Calder's playful inventions from the 1930s onwards, and later in the large-scale, welded pieces of Smith and Anthony Caro.

● Another tactic was to conceive the sculptural form as unusually thin and/or narrow in its dimensions. Here, one thinks of Brancusi's **Bird in Space** of 1919, or of Alberto Giacometti's attenuated, modelled figures from the late 1940s onwards.

● More radical approaches, in technical terms, included assembling a work from planar elements, or even from rod-like forms that read as essentially linear (often described as 'drawing in space'), so that the work appears lighter and less massive than the characteristic products of carving or modelling. Constructed planar sculpture has its point of departure in Pablo Picasso's reliefs like **Guitar** of 1912, and was subsequently elaborated in Cubist sculpture, Tatlin's **Counter-Reliefs**, Constructivist abstraction from the 1920s (e.g. Naum Gabo and Kobro), the welded metal pieces that Picasso and Julio Gonzalez began producing around 1930, and in post war work by Reg Butler, Caro and many others.

● By making such planar or linear elements of transparent glass or plastic, as for instance Gabo did in numerous works from the 1920s onwards, the forms appear even more intangible to the viewer.

● Another way of appearing to defy gravity was to suspend a sculpture from the ceiling, rather than to stand it on a base or directly on the ground. Here, the prime examples that spring to mind are Rodchenko's strongly geometric hanging constructions of 1921 and Calder's many mobiles.

● Finally, the sculpture as a whole might be rendered kinetic, by being imbued with some literal process of motion (through mechanical means) as opposed to the suggestion of movement in, say, a figure sculpture by Auguste Rodin. László Moholy-Nagy's **Light-Space Modulator** (1922-30) is a key early example, while 'Kinetic Sculpture' became a major trend in the 1960s, in the work of figures like Rickey.

In view of the obvious diversity of the work encompassed by these several strategies, it might be wise to look for an underlying coherence not in formal or technical properties as such, but rather in the way these works acted on the viewer. One might argue that, whether it be purely abstract or residually figurative, the sculpture in question counts as 'dematerialised' relative to a norm, consciously or unconsciously applied, which corresponds to the particular physical density of the bodies that we inhabit as we stand in front of, and move around, any given piece of sculpture. Most Western sculpture from antiquity onwards represents, with varying degrees of naturalism, human figures in whose image we intuitively recognise, on the basis of our own sense of bodily identity, a particular interplay of mass and void, sensations of mass and gravity, and a repertoire of possible postures. Sculptural forms may then appear dematerialised, less heavy, solid or opaque, in comparison with this generic expectation. Conversely, forms that seem more heavily-built, so to speak, more densely articulated, or more closely adjusted to an architectural setting, relative again to an internalised bodily norm, might earn the designation of 'monumental', which can perhaps usefully be thought of as the polar opposite of dematerialised. In modern sculpture, much of the work of Henry Moore, for instance, with its tactile invitation and material presence, epitomises the other end of the scale from the ideal of sculptural intangibility. This dichotomy has nothing to do with physical scale; an enormous Caro construction can still come across as immaterial, a small Moore as monumental.

We need to bear in mind a further distinction between the work under scrutiny, with its dematerialisation of form, and the trend towards the so-called 'dematerialisation' of art, or the art object. Confusingly enough, this phrase has often been deployed, in the wake of its launch in a critical essay of 1968, to describe a dominant impulse in art since the mid-1960s. It signifies the way in which the hand-crafted pictorial or sculptural work of art was being supplanted by forms of creative expression that are inherently ephemeral and susceptible to multiple reproduction, such as performance, text, photography, video, site-specific installation, and so forth. Such procedures supposedly offered a challenge to the commodity status of the artwork. In contrast, the works under scrutiny in the present exhibition and essay are traditional sculptural objects, which demand to be displayed, viewed, and even purchased, as one-off pieces.

Having identified dematerialised sculpture as a loose category, and as one strand within the art of a particular period, one might state a further qualification concerning the critical value of the term. Returning to the spectator and the role of projection in perceiving sculpture, one could argue that, in a quite different sense, all sculptural objects possess a dematerialised aspect. In scrutinising a work in the round, as opposed to its photographic reproduction, we characteristically explore and enjoy the interplay between the physical presence and permanence of the three-dimensional configuration in front of us, and the suggestions and sensations it triggers of imagery, movement, texture, formal organisation and so forth, not to mention all manner of feelings, ideas, and associations. In other words, the act of looking at any piece of sculpture will tend to involve a certain process of dematerialisation, an interpretation by the viewer that includes, but also goes significantly beyond, acknowledging the mere material from which the object is made. It is in this process that the work, as it were, comes to life, in representational and aesthetic terms. Worthwhile sculptures sustain a complex and stimulating oscillation between, broadly speaking, physical and imaginative readings, a point that surely applies just as much to a transparent, plastic construction from the 1920s as it does to Michelangelo's **David**. In this respect, dematerialisation seems a misleading term, suggesting as it does the devaluing of direct, material sensation. Such implications underpinned the flawed, yet highly influential, account given by the New York critic Rosalind Krauss in her book *Passages in Modern Sculpture* (1977). This identified, in the work of artists like Gabo, "a kind of sculptural idealism" and an impulse towards "the revelation of a transcendent reality rather than a manifestation of factual reality", supposed characteristics that could be played off, to good rhetorical effect, against the allegedly less cerebral, more phenomenological responses, in relation to the specifics of material and site, that were solicited by the work of her own contemporaries (and friends) such as Carl Andre, Robert Morris, and Richard Serra.[3] In reality, a dematerialised sculpture is just as material in its impact on the senses, albeit in a different way, as a very literal and emphatic presentation of some physical substance.

3. Rosalind Krauss, *Passages in Modern Sculpture*, Cambridge, Mass., and London 1977, p. 57 and passim. The continuing influence of Krauss's treatment is evident in Alex Potts, *The Sculptural Imagination*, New Haven and London 2000, where the analysis of Gabo, for instance, is disappointing (pp. 108-109). Conversely, Potts's extended treatment of the work of Carl Andre (Chapter 9) is a model of the approach to sculpture advocated here for work from the earlier part of the century.

It may be as well, finally, to reiterate the point that immaterial sculptures are markedly diverse. There are some shared strategies and conventions, as we have seen, but the resulting works seem, in more telling ways, to spring from quite contradictory motives and intentions. Beyond extreme attenuation, a Brancusi **Bird in Space** and a Giacometti **Standing Figure** have very little in common. The same can be said of the constructed sculptures that Gonzalez and Gabo made in the 1920s and 1930s. It seems desirable, therefore, to progress from the general to the particular, and to excavate the specific concerns of individuals. To this end, we shall focus on Naum Gabo (1890-1977), whose work is well represented in the present exhibition. Gabo's approach manifests several aspects of the wider project of divesting sculpture of its traditional materiality, and opens up several points of contact with the experiments of his contemporaries.[4] Considering his development in chronological terms, to begin with, will serve to indicate the sequence of interests and stimuli that informed his creation of a remarkable body of 'dematerialised' sculpture – not to mention the two-dimensional elaborations of his sculptural idiom, such as paintings and prints, which are also included in the show.

The bulk of Gabo's sculptures are constructed from cut-out planes, which may be flat or curved, opaque or transparent. It is evident from **Torso** (c.1917; see cat. no. 24) that, like many other sculptors in the 1910s, Gabo initially extrapolated this planar method from studying Cubist painting. In the early figurative sculptures, he projected fairly complex forms as open volumes penetrated by space, rather than as solid masses. The armature of interlocking and receding planes creates an intricate honeycomb of pockets of shadow, against which the outer edges catch the light, and in their rhythmical continuities imply the absent surface or skin. In order to create his constructions, Gabo seems to have initially experimented with card or thin plastic planes, which led eventually to the making of a precise template from which the finished sculptures could be produced at any scale, in any suitable material, and whenever he saw fit. In the case of **Torso**, he may have made small models during the First World War, when he was living in Norway to escape the fighting and avoid conscription into the Tsar's army. The 1917 Revolution enabled him to return home to Russia, and he proceeded to create a large iron **Torso** (lost, presumed destroyed) in time for a group exhibition in Moscow in 1920.

4. The discussion that follows draws on Martin Hammer and Christina Lodder, *Constructing Modernity. The Art and Career of Naum Gabo*, New Haven and London 2000.

The show was Gabo's first public appearance as a sculptor and the occasion for publicising his artistic philosophy in *The Realistic Manifesto.*[5] He asserted the scientific and technological resonances of his art: "With a plumb line in the hand, with eyes as precise as a ruler, with a spirit as taut as a compass, we build them in the same way as the universe builds its own creations, as the engineer his bridges, as the mathematician his formulae of the orbits".[6] In particular, Gabo associated the idea of building or constructing sculptural form with the dematerialising, economical approaches to structure that had come to the fore in modern engineering:

> We reject in sculpture mass as a sculptural element.
> Every engineer has known for a long time that the static force of bodies, their material strength, does not depend on their mass. For example: a rail, a flying buttress, a girder, etc.[7]

Gabo's models were engineering components like the steel T- and I-beams, which were lightweight and narrow in section but strong under compression. **Torso** perhaps echoes the cantilevered form of cranes, or even the tapering contours and horizontal divisions of the Eiffel Tower of 1889, that supreme example of an elegant, monumental form, which was visibly constructed from slender girders, allowing the free passage of space within the form.

The arrival of electricity at around the same time drove an even more dramatic wedge between notions of force and physical substance. New means of transport and communication were powered by invisible, dynamic energies, and machinery provided a further example of solid form transmuted into immaterial forces. In particular, it was Gabo's familiarity with experimental laboratory equipment, from his scientific studies at Munich University before the war, that lay behind the conception in Moscow of **Kinetic Construction (Standing Wave)** (c.1920; cat. no. 25). More a demonstration than a sculpture in its own right, this work comprises a thin metal rod, which is caused to vibrate by a motor, and which through its oscillations describes a virtual volume or wave-like form in space. To an extreme degree, form is separated from material structure. The metaphorical connotations of

5. Translations by both Gabo and the editors in Martin Hammer and Christina Lodder (Eds.), *Gabo on Gabo: Texts and Interviews*, Forest Row 2000, pp. 21-35.
6. *Ibid.*, p. 32.
7. *Ibid.*, p. 33.

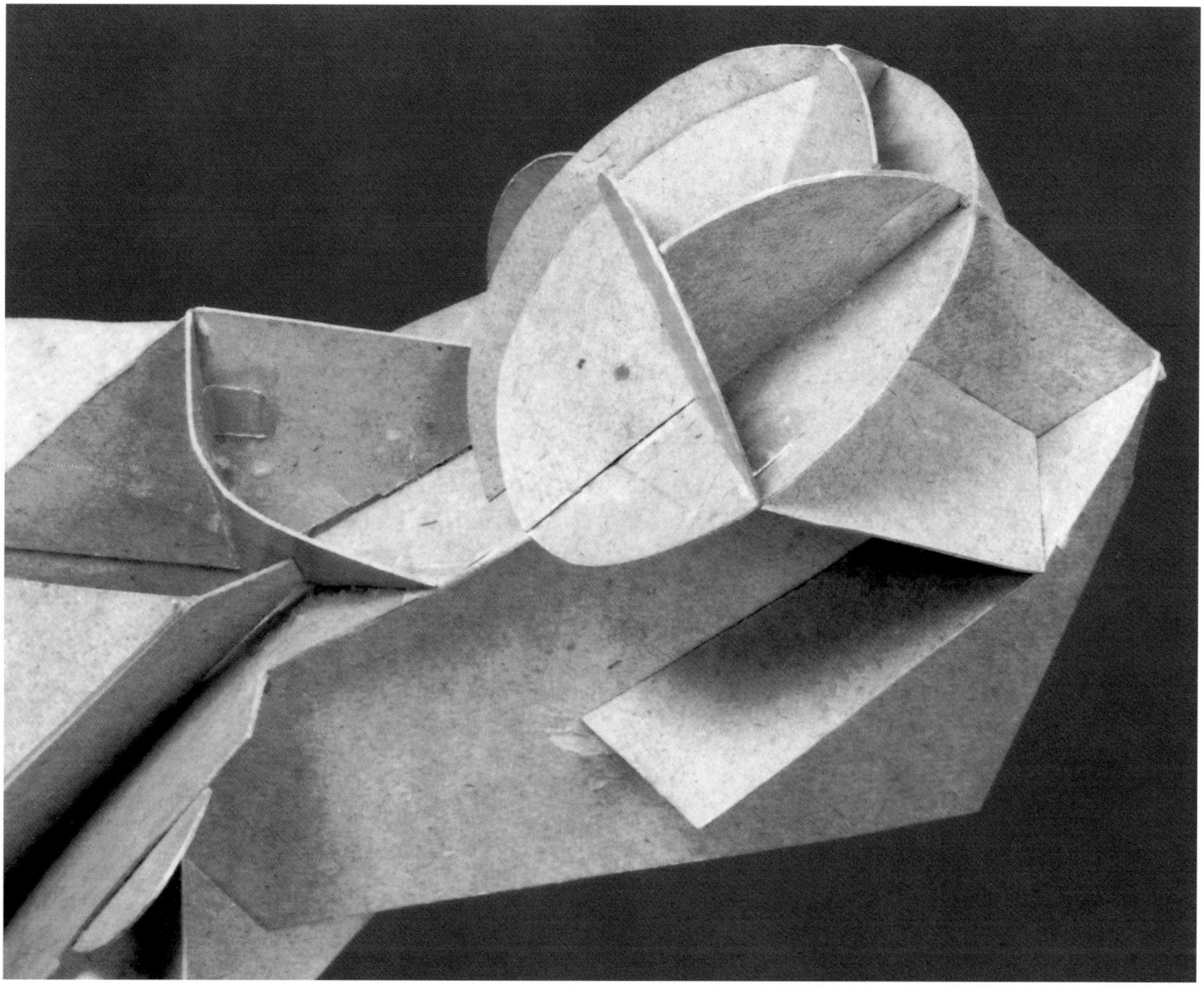

Naum Gabo
Model for 'Constructed Torso' (detail)
1917 (reassembled 1981)   Cat. No. 24

such an image were wide-ranging. On one level, for instance, the project may have seemed to distil the ideas of the French philosopher Henri Bergson, who was so admired by Gabo and his contemporaries. For Bergson, the division of time into separate moments is akin to the perception of spatial reality in terms of distinct solids. Such 'commonsensical' concepts are in fact mere projections of the intellect, which is geared towards practical existence. At a deeper, more intuitive level, man's inner sense of time comprises duration, an undivided flux of sensations, memories, and emotions. Likewise, the material world is characterised by "flux, a continuity of flowing, a becoming".[8] According to Bergson, "life is an evolution ... What is real is the continual *change of* form: *form is only a snapshot view of a transition* ... our perception manages to solidify into discontinuous images the fluid continuity of the real".[9] It is a short step to Gabo's assertion that "time is continuous in its real duration", and his contemptuous dismissal of Futurist depictions of movement through time: "It is obvious to anyone that by a simple graphic recording of a sequence of momentary snapshots of arrested movement you cannot recreate movement itself".[10] **Kinetic Construction** intimates in sculptural terms a Bergsonian sense of continuous time and energy.

The radical art of the Russian avant-garde, Kazimir Malevich's Suprematism and the proto-Constructivist experiments of Tatlin and his followers, prompted artists such as Gabo and Moholy-Nagy to dispense with subject matter and to begin experimenting with pure abstraction. Moholy-Nagy's **Light-Space Modulator**, for example, marks a further development of the kinetic ideal. The projection of lights onto the construction, creating strong shadows, reinforces the intricate interplay between material and immaterial. Moreover the whole construction is made to rotate on its circular base, and the individual elements, simple geometric forms made from polished metal and glass, perform a complex ballet in space. Moholy-Nagy even planned to synchronise the movements of the construction with a musical score. **Light-Space Modulator** evokes the idealisation of technological, scientific and, potentially, social progress that emerged in response to the cataclysmic destruction of the First World War, and to the beacon of hope represented at this stage by the

8. Henri Bergson, *Creative Evolution*, London 1911, p. 390. Originally published in 1907, and subsequently translated into Russian.
9. *Ibid.*, p. 319.
10. Naum Gabo and Antoine Pevsner, *The Realistic Manifesto*, republished in M. Hammer and C. Lodder, *op. cit.*, p. 30.

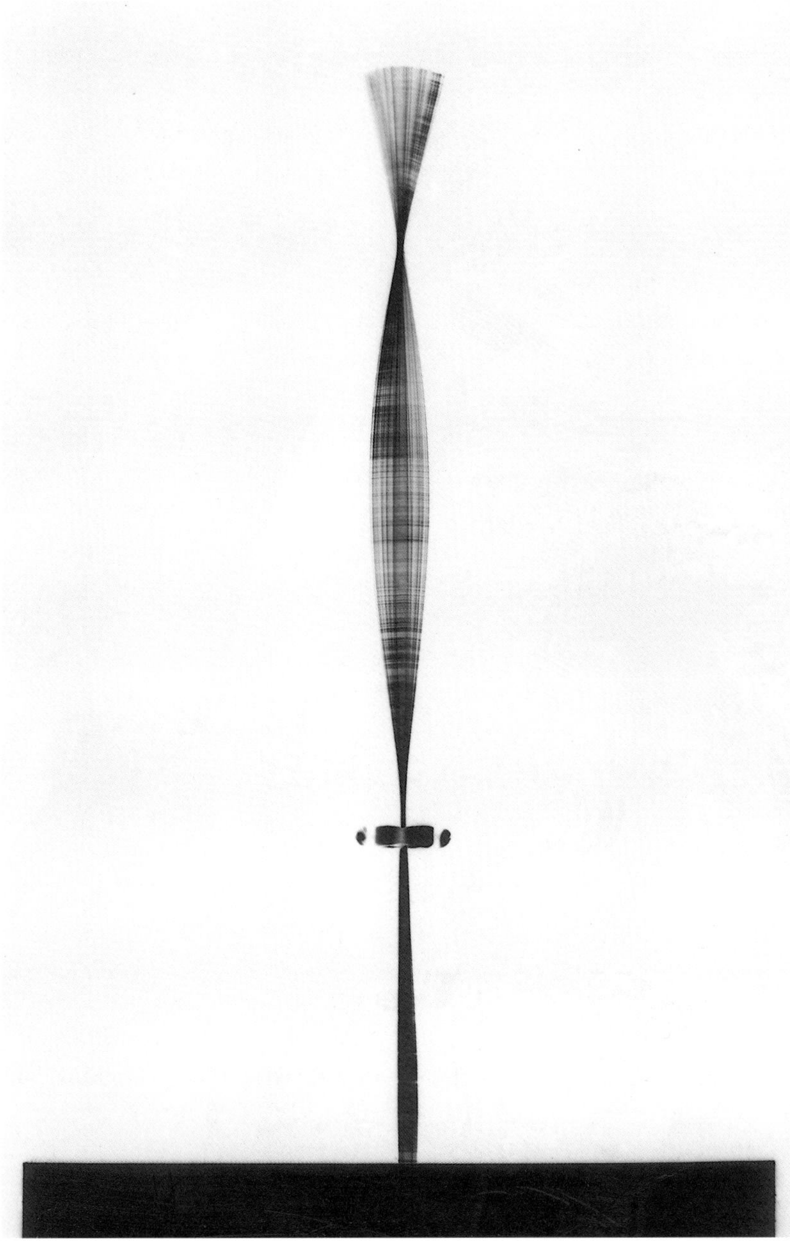

Naum Gabo
Kinetic Construction (Standing Wave)
1919-20 (replica 1985) Cat. No. 25

Russian Revolution. In his 1922 essay, *Constructivism and the Proletariat*, Moholy-Nagy announced: "To be a user of the machine is to be of the spirit of this century. It has replaced the transcendental spiritualism of past eras. Before the machine, everyone is equal ... There is no tradition in technology, no consciousness of class or standing ... This is the root of socialism."[11]

Gabo undoubtedly shared this utopian outlook, but in practice he found mechanical technology too limiting and obtrusive, when it came to developing more elaborate sculptural forms, and he tended to rely on fictive sensations of movement. A case in point is **Construction in Space with Balance on Two Points** (1925; cat. no. 26), which typifies the remarkable body of purely abstract constructions that Gabo produced after moving to Berlin in 1922 from an increasingly authoritarian Soviet Russia, just as Moholy-Nagy had come to Germany the previous year in the wake of the failed revolution in Hungary. In **Balance on Two Points**, the form reads as a complex geometrical figure transposed into three dimensions. Visually, the work's most striking quality is its apparent denial of gravity and solid structural support. As the title implies, the entire construction is balanced on just two points at its base, to either side of the central vertical axis. Immediately above, the cube, implied by the four white rectangular planes, appears to hover in space, while its 45° orientation suggests the possibility of rotation. Crucial to this entire effect is the inclusion of precisely cut transparent glass and plastic planes. Gabo began to use such materials extensively once he had access to the more sophisticated technical and industrial resources of the West. The physical surfaces only register in terms of reflections, and it is the edges that catch and refract the light, generating immaterial, luminous lines that appear to define and enclose configurations of space.

Gabo's explorations of transparent materials and open, planar structures, suggesting the continuous, uninterrupted flow of space, recall the concerns of a new generation of progressive architects who, according to Walter Gropius in 1925, "affirm the world of today, with its machines, with its motorised transport and its tempo. They are striving for ever bolder creative means to overcome gravity itself, to achieve by new techniques, both in appearance and reality, a state of hovering above

11. L. Moholy-Nagy, "Constructivism and the Proletariat" (1922), in Tim and Charlotte Benton with Dennis Sharp (Eds.), *Form and Function: A Source Book for the History of Architecture and Design 1890-1939*, London 1975, p. 95.

the ground".[12] The increased emphasis on glass as an architectural element was made possible by the use of the steel frame. In 1929, the Berlin architect Arthur Korn writing about the 'new glass age', asserted that "it is now possible to have an independent wall of glass around a building; no longer a solid wall with windows".[13] Gabo's series of tower constructions, particularly **Column**, conceived in Moscow but realised in Berlin, possess an especially strong architectonic resonance. They read as miniaturised sculptural equivalents to the projects for tall buildings that were being produced in the early 1920s. The emphasis on transparency in **Column** brings to mind Mies van der Rohe's glazed skyscraper projects, while the cruciform plan comprising two intersected glass planes may be compared with Le Corbusier's imaginary tower blocks for his futuristic *Contemporary City*. Gabo certainly knew Mies, who was also based in Berlin and moving in the same circles around the avant-garde magazine *G: Material zur elementaren Gestaltung*.

During the 1930s, Gabo's formal vocabulary became increasingly organic and curvilinear, and the associations with mechanical imagery and architectural structures fell away. For Gabo, this development was certainly facilitated by his discovery of Perspex after his arrival in England in 1936. First marketed by I.C.I. in 1935, as a replacement for safety glass in car windscreens, Perspex had a more pristine transparency than earlier plastics such as Celluloid, and, when heated, could more readily be twisted and bent into curved planes. **Construction on a Line** (1937; cat. no. 27) was one of Gabo's first experiments with Perspex, and represented an inventive rethinking of the relief format, which would conventionally have been built up from the ground plane, or else cut or carved back into the depth of the plane, in the manner of his friend Ben Nicholson's white reliefs. Gabo's innovation was to use a square sheet of transparent plastic as the ground plane. This allowed him to develop a dynamic, highly immaterial composition on the frontal plane itself, and also projecting both backwards and forwards in relation to the virtually invisible ground. The result is highly 'pictorial'; for a viewer standing directly in front of the sculpture, it is very difficult to gauge its literal depth and to determine which elements are physically situated in front of the ground plane and which behind.

12. Walter Gropius, *Internationale Architektur*, Munich 1925, translation "International Architecture", in Charlotte and Tim Benton (Eds.), *Images*, Milton Keynes 1975, p. 4.
13. Arthur Korn, *Glas im Bau und als Gebrauchsgegenstand*, Berlin 1929, translation "Glass in Modern Architecture", in T. Benton, et al., *Form and Function*, p. 170.

Gabo's subsequent, radically transparent constructions in the round are exemplified in this exhibition by **Spiral Theme** (cat. no. 28), created in 1941 when Gabo and his wife were living in Carbis Bay, Cornwall, whence they, Nicholson and Barbara Hepworth had all retreated after the outbreak of the Second World War. **Spiral Theme** suggests that Gabo could even derive stimulation from watching mobile light images on the wall, created by reflections from shiny surfaces. He made a series of photographs of such phenomena in 1941 (cat no. 37 a-e), and some of the resulting configurations seem to have fed into the sculpture he was working on at the time. In the final work, the lines and the luminous, white edges of the planes (another striking feature of Perspex as opposed to glass), trace a complex movement around the small spring-like form at the centre, creating rhythmical configurations in space which appear beautifully poised from different angles and heights of viewpoint. Ultimately, the taut geometry of **Spiral Theme** is very different from the loose, playful, and free-flowing idiom that Moholy-Nagy would explore in **Spirals** and **Leda and the Swan** (both 1946; cat. nos. 57 and 58). Like many cultural figures who fled from Nazi Germany, Moholy had moved to America before the war, and it was there that he too turned to Perspex (or Plexiglas) as a material with exciting sculptural possibilities.

Gabo's pursuit of immateriality found further elaboration in the linear constructions that he embarked upon in Cornwall, employing a nylon filament that was, once again, fresh on the market as a substitute for silk. His use of stringing is very different from that developed, probably a little earlier, by Hepworth and Moore. In their work a cast or carved form tends to be dominant and the threads are more widely spaced and register as individual linear elements, played against the solid elements. In contrast, Gabo wound the almost colourless nylon filament around a more neutral, notched framework of clear Perspex, with the threads clustered sufficiently closely together to create the illusion of continuous, taut parabolic forms, which at the same time are visibly permeated by space. In **Linear Construction No.2** (1950; see cat. no. 29), created after his final uprooting to the United States in 1946, the stringing evokes layered, interpenetrating forms around the underlying structure of two inverted, transparent planes. The intangibility of the form is reinforced by the transformations in the pattern of reflections that occur with every slight shift in the orientation of the viewer. Moreover, Gabo soon conceived a version of the sculpture that was suspended from the ceiling by wire, enabling the construction to move and turn very slightly, in response to currents of

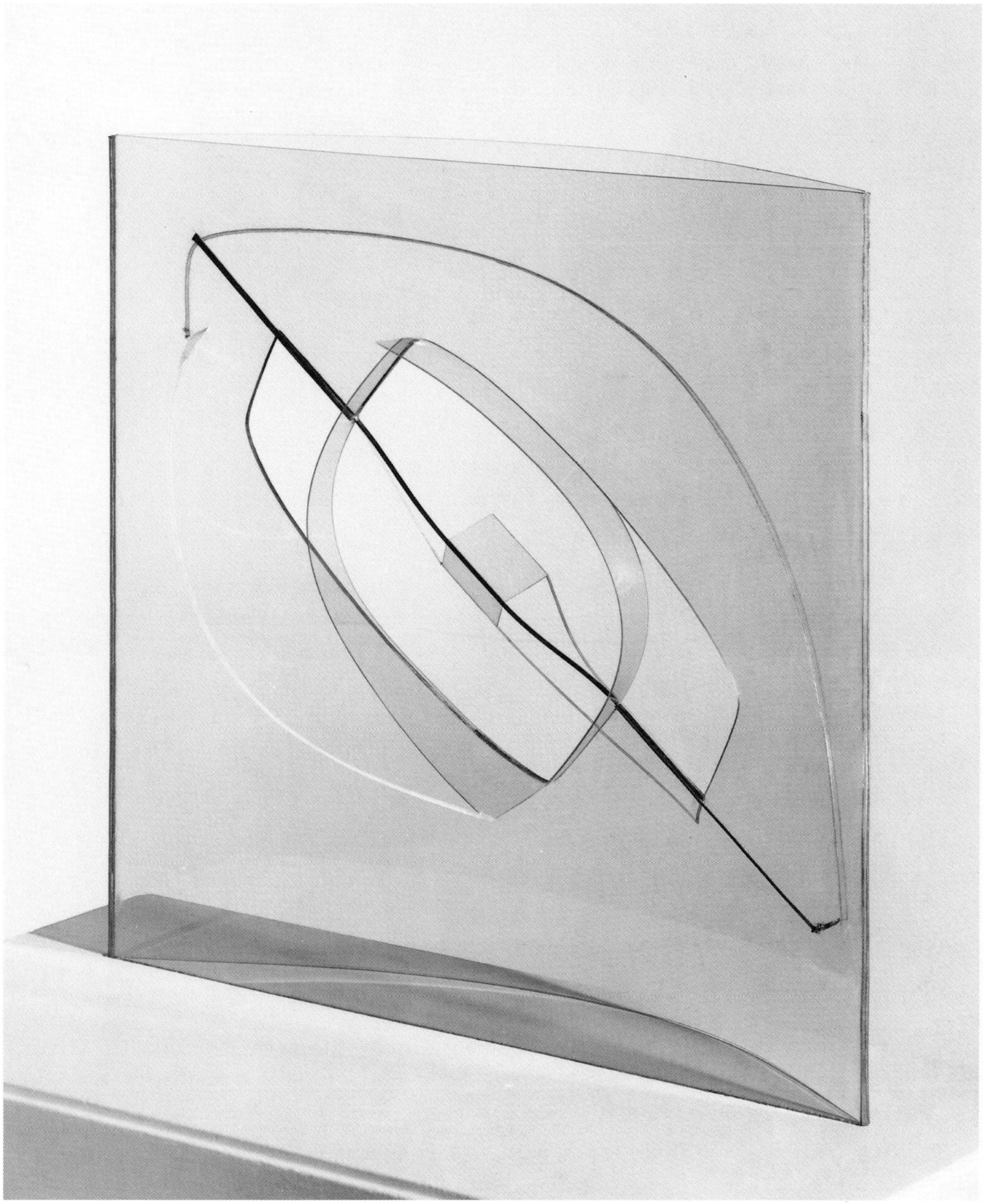

Naum Gabo
Construction on a Line
1935-37 Cat. No. 27

air, creating a shimmer of reflected highlights. He intended the sculpture to hover an inch or two above a base. This was partly for protection, but the solidity of the base also prevents the sculpture appearing to hang heavily in space. Indeed, the overall effect of the sculpture is remarkably intangible, refuting the conventional identification between a sculpture and a physical object that the viewer might imaginatively grasp and touch.

It was also in 1950 that Gabo began to experiment with wood-engraving, stimulated by his friendship with William Ivins, retired curator of prints at the Metropolitan Museum, New York, and now a neighbour of Gabo's in Connecticut. This very traditional medium might appear incongruous, given Gabo's use of highly contemporary materials for his constructions. But his approach to printmaking was in fact a direct extension of his sculptural concerns. The simple, mainly linear designs that he cut into the blocks are made, in the eventual monoprints, to float against dark, mottled grounds, with the white lines echoing the effect of light seeming to glow along the edges of Perspex planes (cat nos. 30-36). Gabo found that he preferred working on thin tissue, and would occasionally even mount the prints between two sheets of clear plastic, so that they might be held up or hung against the light.

What meanings did Gabo intend to convey by means of the remarkably delicate and transparent effects that infused his art? As an antidote to Krauss's assertion that physical sensations are subordinate to concepts in his work, we might note his own repeated declarations that constructed sculpture was concerned to heighten the viewer's sense of pure space, conceived as something independent from solid form:

> We consider it [space] as an 'absolute sculptural element', released from any closed volume, and we represent it from inside with its own specific properties.
>
> I do not hesitate to affirm that the perception of space is a primary natural sense which belongs to the basic senses of our psychology ...
>
> Our task is to penetrate deeper into its substance and bring it closer to our consciousness; so that the sensation of space will become for us a more elementary and everyday emotion the same as the sensation of light or the sensation of sound.
>
> In our sculpture space has ceased to be for us a logical abstraction or a transcendental idea and has become a malleable material element.[14]

14. Gabo, "Sculpture: Carving and Construction in Space", in J. L. Martin, Ben Nicholson, N. Gabo (Eds.), *Circle*, London 1937, p. 107.

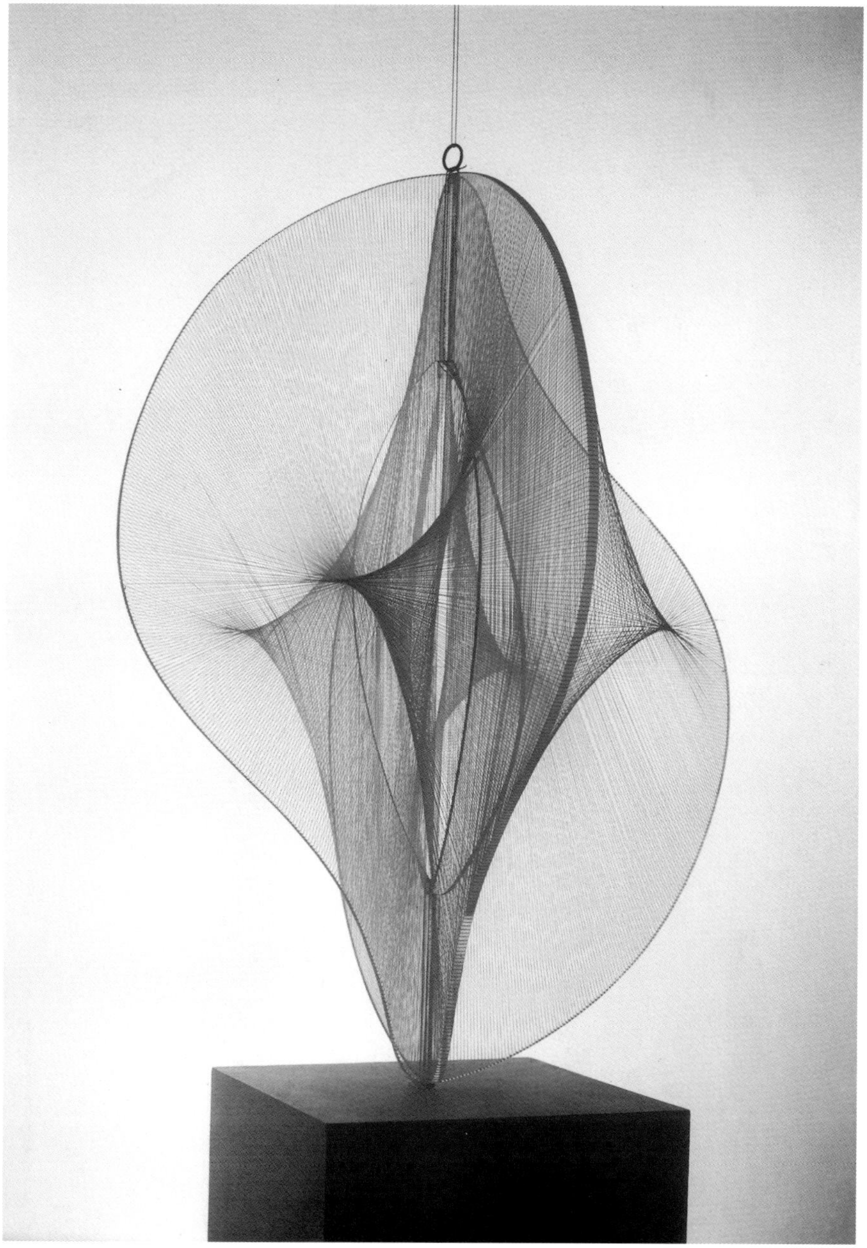

Naum Gabo
Linear Construction No.2
1970-71 Cat. No. 29

Gabo's emphasis on the reality and immediacy of spatial experience was not just aesthetic in origin. He believed that his work epitomised a convergence between directions in the visual arts and in the wider intellectual environment: "I would say that the philosophic events and the events in science at the beginning of this century have definitely made a crucial impact on the mentality of my generation. Whether many of us knew exactly what was going on in science, or not, does not really matter. The fact was that it was in the air, and an artist, with his sensitiveness, acts like a sponge".[15] The nature of Gabo's studies meant that he was actually in a better position than most artists to know about contemporary science. It was in a lecture he gave at Yale University in 1948 that he provided his most specific account of the contemporary scientific thinking that corresponded to the sensations of dematerialisation and dynamic rhythm transmitted by his constructions. Wary of being seen as a mere illustrator of the new theories, he presented them as a justification, by analogy, for his own artistic departures from 'commonsensical' ways of understanding and representing external reality:

> ... when our contemporary sciences are developing an image of the world so entirely different from both the previous ones as to appear to us almost absurd, incomprehensible to common sense, we are again willing to take it – we have already accepted it; we have gotten familiar with a world in which forces are permitted to become mass and matter is permitted to become light; a world which is pictured to us as a conglomeration of oscillating electrons, protons, neutrons, particles which behave like waves, which in their turn behave like particles. If the scientist is permitted to picture to us an image of an electron which under certain conditions has less than zero energy (in common language, it means that it weighs less than nothing) and if he is permitted to see behind this simple common table, an image of the curvature of space – why, may I ask, is not the contemporary artist to be permitted to search for and bring forward an image of the world more in accordance with the achievements of our developed mind, even if it is different from the image presented in the paintings and sculptures of our predecessors?[16]

15. Gabo, "Russia and Constructivism", in Hammer and Lodder, *Gabo on Gabo*, cit., p. 213 (interview published in 1957).
16. Gabo, "On Constructive Realism" (1948 lecture), in Hammer and Lodder, *Gabo on Gabo*, cit., pp. 76-77.

Such remarks confirm that Gabo possessed at least a rudimentary knowledge of advanced modern physics. In 1911, Ernest Rutherford had shown that the internal structure of atoms comprised electrons and protons orbiting around a nucleus, and in 1932 James Chadwick had demonstrated that this nucleus contained a neutron. The interchangeability of waves and particles, for descriptive purposes, was central to the Quantum Mechanics developed by Planck, Heisenberg and others during the 1920s. Paul Dirac showed in 1928 that if quantum theory was made to conform to special relativity, the mathematics generated negative energy states. We know that Gabo owned a copy of Sir James Jeans's *The Mysterious Universe*, first published in 1930, where the current scientific consensus was summarised as follows:

> ... for ever solid matter melts into insubstantial radiation: for ever the tangible changes into the intangible ... the tendency of modern physics is to resolve the whole universe into waves ... These waves are of two kinds: bottled-up waves, which we call matter, and unbottled waves, which we call radiation or light ... it no longer seems surprising that the fundamental particles of which matter is built should exhibit many of the properties of waves.[17]

How did the constructions themselves convey Gabo's awareness of scientific theory? In general terms, the sculptural sensations of movement and space permeating form provided a distillation of the new scientific paradigm, whereby the physical universe was understood in terms of fields of forces and energies, and familiar distinctions between 'solid' matter and 'empty' space no longer pertained. More specifically, the curvilinear language of form characteristic of Gabo's work after 1930 may well have been intended to evoke the inherently curved nature of space. Spatial curvature became a central principle of modern physics, although it is not an easy idea to grasp or visualise, and it contradicts the commonsensical idea that the three-dimensional space in which we act is defined by the rectilinear coordinates of vertical and horizontal. Einstein's general theory of relativity of 1915, had established that the physical universe exists not within absolute space and absolute time, conceived separately from one another, but rather within a dynamic space-time continuum, a system conforming to the principles of spatial curvature in Non-Euclidean geometry. To quote Jeans's trenchant summary:

> ... this theory tells us that space itself is curved, much in the same way in which the surface of the earth is curved. The curvature of space is

17. Sir James Jeans, *The Mysterious Universe*, Cambridge 1930, pp. 97-99. Gabo owned the 1937 reprint.

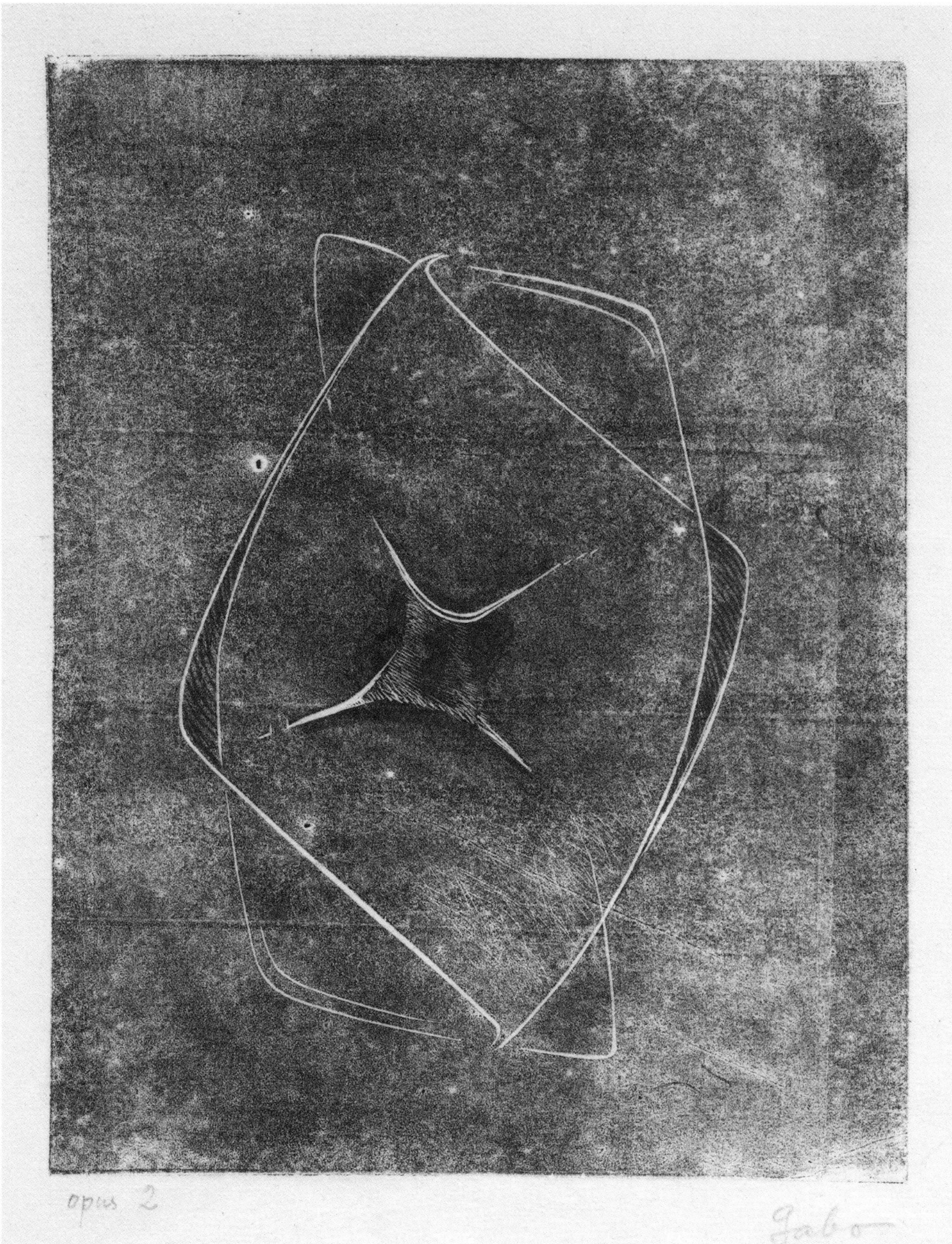

Naum Gabo
Opus 2
1950 Cat. No. 31

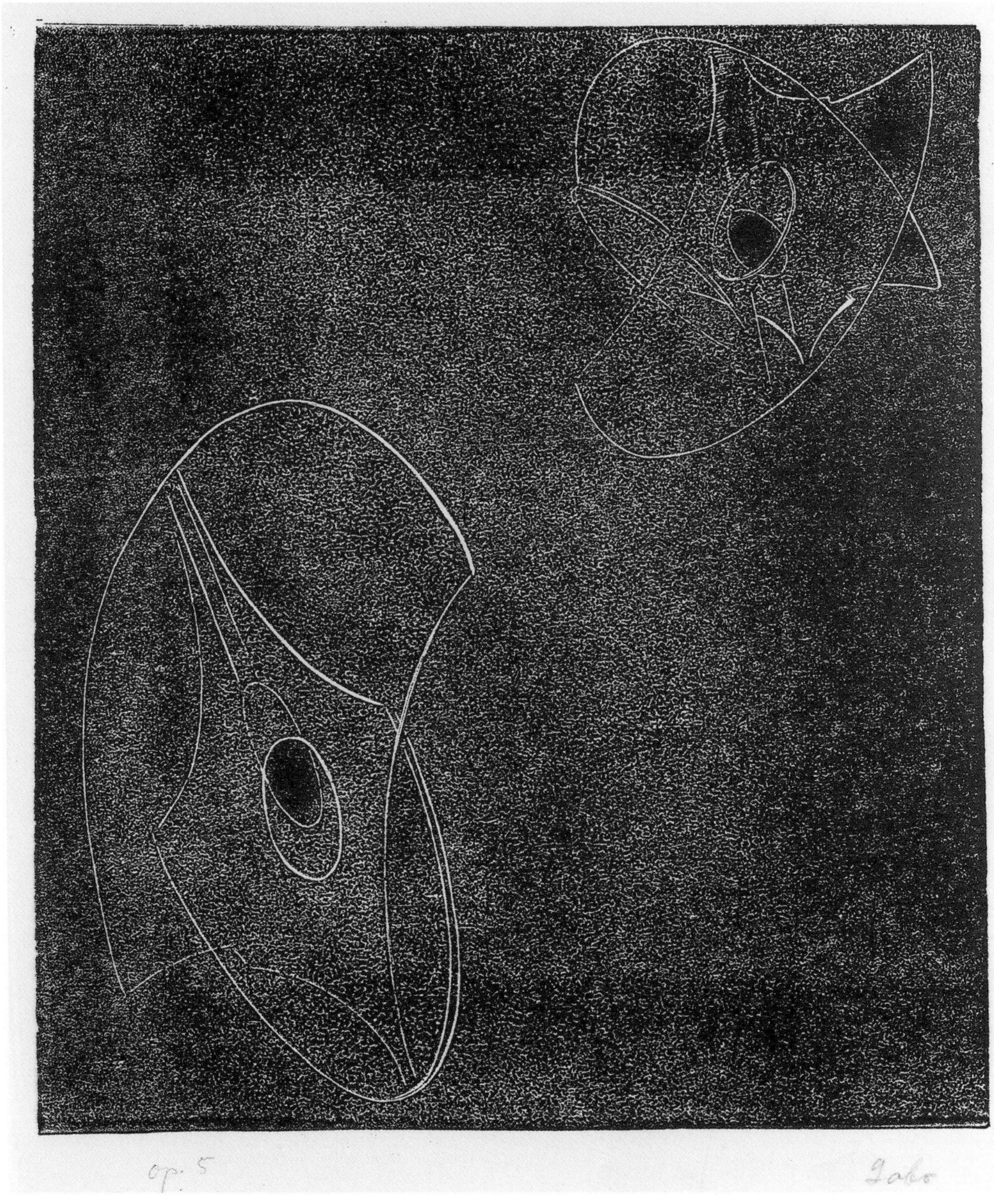

Naum Gabo
Opus 5
1950 Cat. No. 35

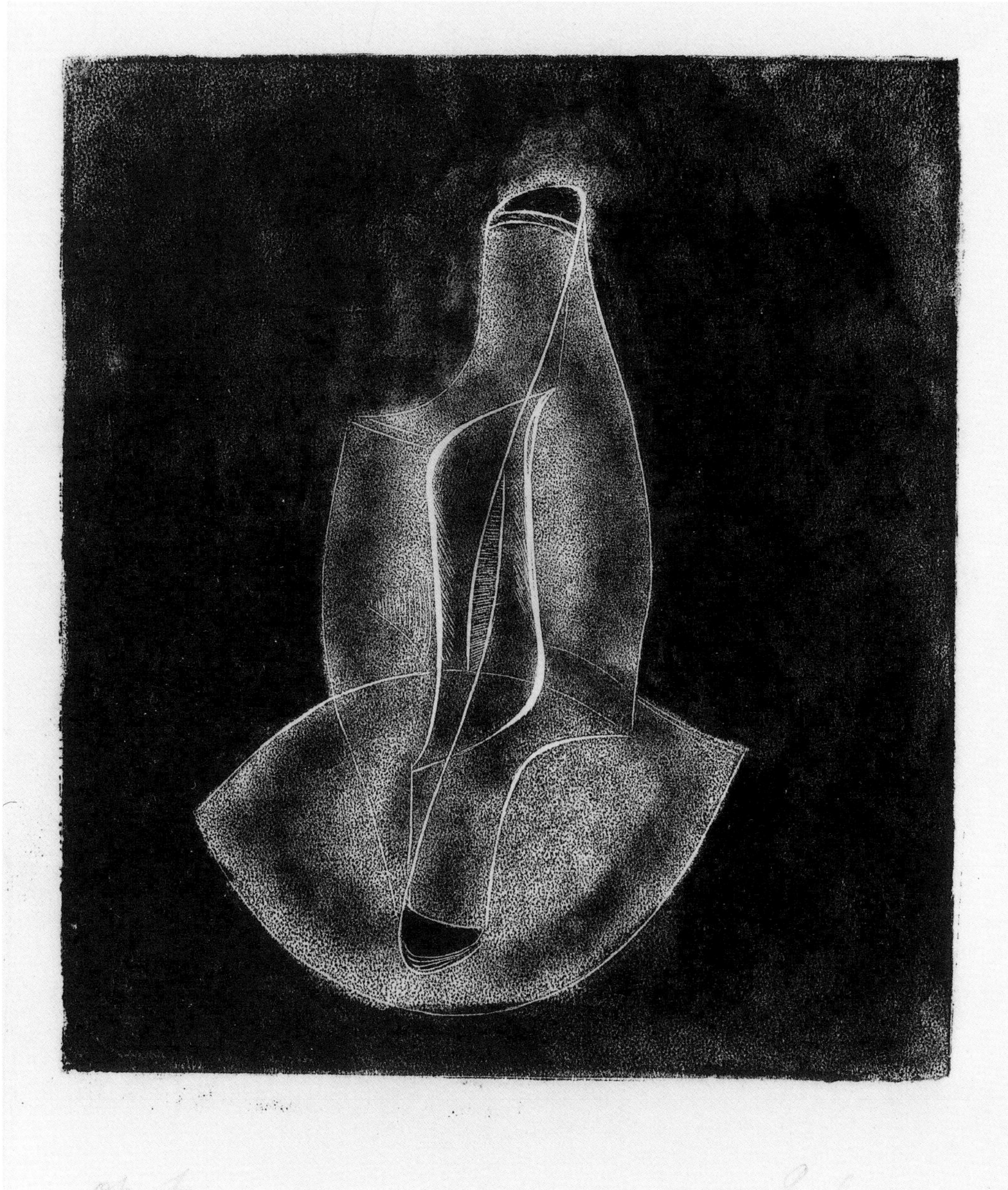

Naum Gabo
Opus 4
1950 Cat. No. 32

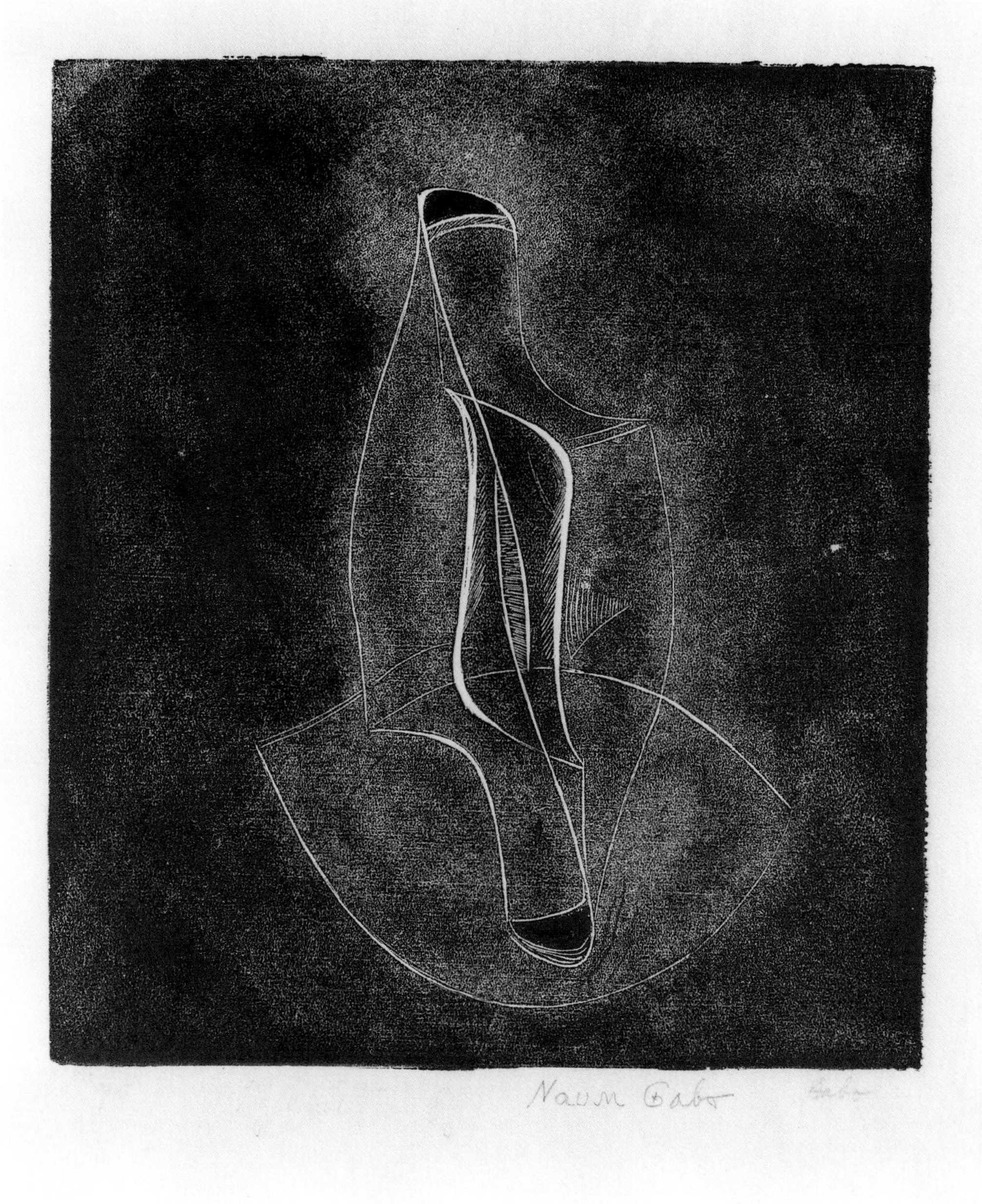

Naum Gabo
Opus 4
1950 Cat. No. 33

> responsible for the curving of rays of light which is observed at a solar eclipse, and for the curvature in the paths of planets and comets, which we used to attribute to a 'force' of gravitation. On this theory, the presence of matter does not produce 'force', which is an illusion, but a curving of space ... The more matter there is in the universe, the more curved space will be, the more rapidly it will bend back on itself.[18]

The final sentence especially brings to mind Gabo's **Spheric Theme**, arguably the most extreme manifestation of his impulse to eliminate rectilinear form. By the time he conceived the work around 1937 he had also acquired Sir Arthur Eddington's *The Expanding Universe* (1933), with its chapter devoted to 'Spherical Space'.[19] It was perhaps to such fairly accessible accounts that Gabo was referring in his later commentary on the genesis of this construction, where he indicates more specifically than anywhere else how the creation of his sculpture might be informed by reading and thinking about contemporary science:

> I felt that the visual character of space is not angular; that to transfer the perception of space into sculptural terms, it has to be spheric. I was looking for an indication in the scientific world, where a method of spheric structure could perhaps be found.
>
> I found no answer in graphic terms in science which would satisfy my vision of space. I consider that in this work of mine there is a satisfactory solution to that problem. Instead of indicating space by an angular intersection of planes, I enclose the space in one curved continuous surface.[20]

Gabo's experiments with new materials, with the language of constructed form, and with suggestions of movement, were not, therefore, merely driven by formalist imperatives. His decisions were also informed by an ambition to "bring forward an image of the world more in accordance with the achievements of our developed mind". It was reality itself that now seemed fundamentally incompatible with old ideas of solid, static volume. The task facing the artist, in the view of Gabo and like-minded artists such as Moholy-Nagy, was nothing less than distilling and conveying to a wider public the exciting new understanding of time, space, and matter in modern science and philosophy.

18. *Ibid.*, p. 53.
19. Sir Arthur Eddington, *The Expanding Universe*, Harmondsworth 1940 (first published in 1933).
20. N. Gabo, in Hammer and Lodder, *Gabo on Gabo*, cit., p. 223 (originally published in 1957).

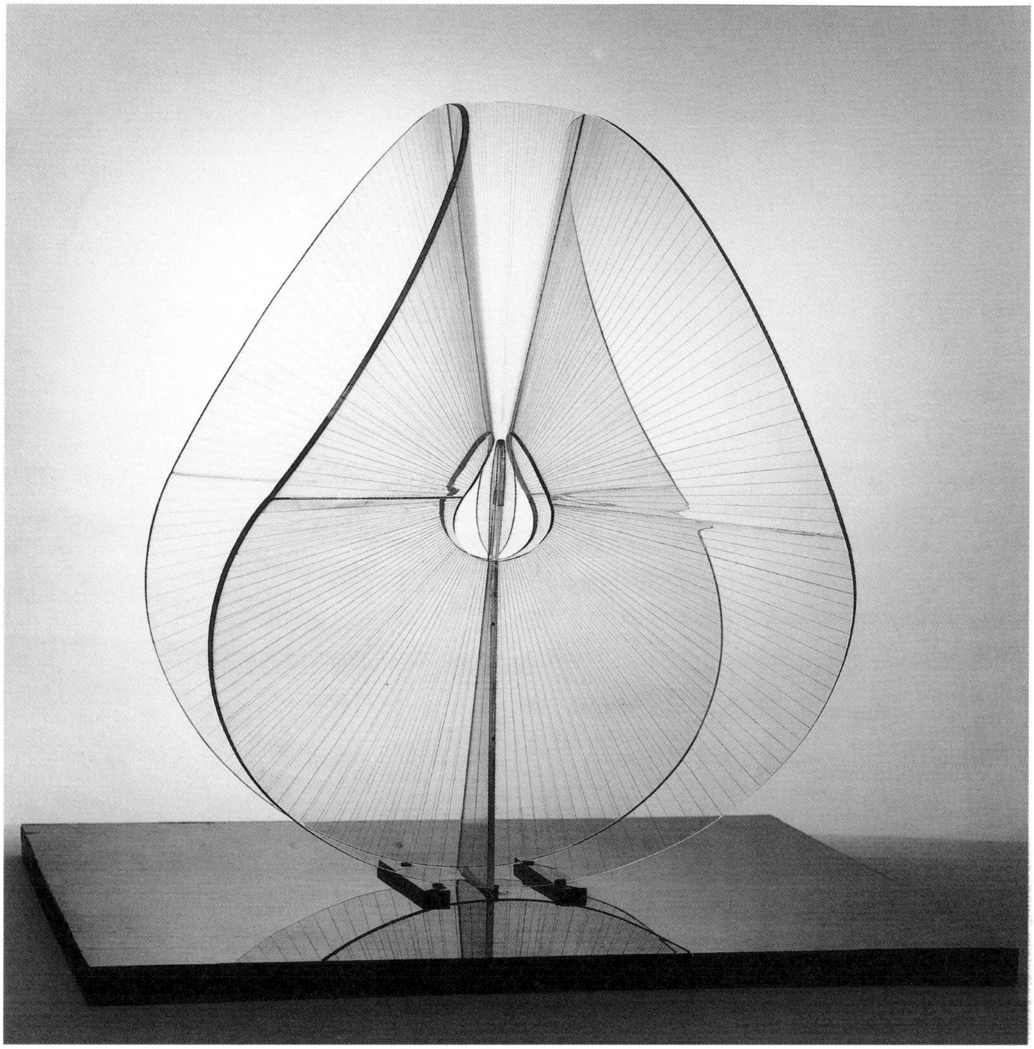

Naum Gabo
Spheric Theme: Translucent Variation
1951
Collection The Solomon R. Guggenheim Museum, New York

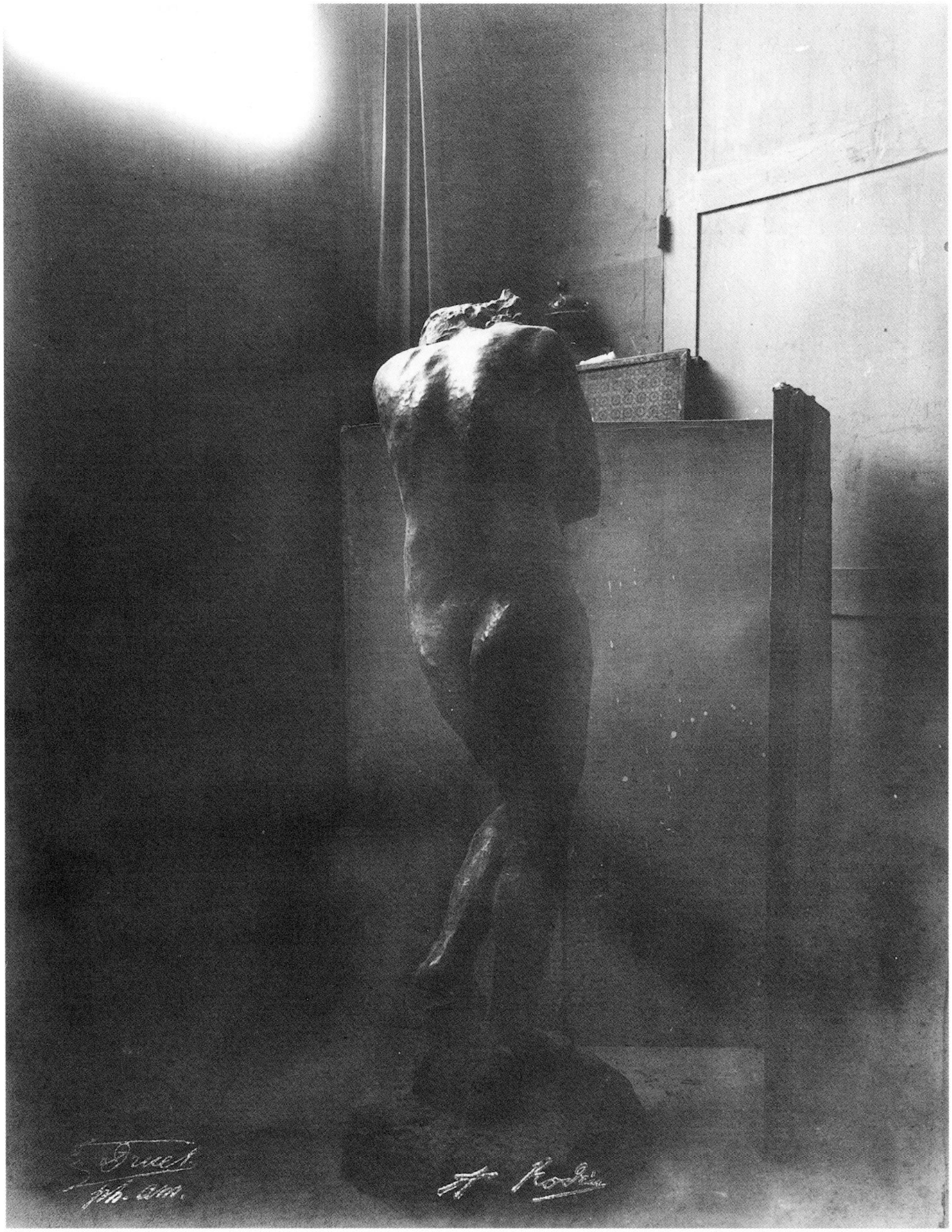

Eugène Druet
Eve
c. 1899 Cat. No. 4

"AN ALMOST IMMATERIAL SUBSTANCE": PHOTOGRAPHY AND THE DEMATERIALISATION OF SCULPTURE

Geraldine A. Johnson

Some of the earliest known photographs depict sculptural subjects.[1] But most of the photographs taken in the decades immediately following the discovery of the new medium served primarily documentary purposes. Only in the later nineteenth century did sculptors and photographers begin to explore how photography could be used not just to record the external appearance of three-dimensional objects, but also to question long-held assumptions about the art of sculpture itself. In fact, beginning with Auguste Rodin, a number of artists began to deploy the medium to explore the very nature of sculpture's materiality.

Rodin

From the mid-1870s onwards, Rodin actively incorporated photography into his artistic practices, with the medium becoming increasingly important in the design, marketing and documentation of his sculptural oeuvre.[2] His imaginatively varied use of photography became a model for both immediate contemporaries, such as Medardo Rosso, and somewhat younger artists working in the first decades of the twentieth century, including László Moholy-Nagy, Naum Gabo and Constantin

1. On the photography of sculpture, see: Geraldine A. Johnson (Ed.), *Sculpture and Photography: Envisioning the Third Dimension*, Cambridge 1998, esp. p. 16, n. 2, for further references; James Hall, *The World as Sculpture*, London 1999, pp. 325-347; and Dorothy Kosinski, *The Artist and the Camera: Degas to Picasso*, New Haven 1999, *passim*.
2. On Rodin and photography, see: Albert E. Elsen, *In Rodin's Studio: A photographic record of sculpture in the making*, Oxford 1980; Kirk Varnedoe, "Rodin and Photography", in A.E. Elsen (Ed.), *Rodin Rediscovered*, Washington D.C. 1981, pp. 202-247; Hélène Pinet, "'Montrer est la question vitale': Rodin and Photography", in Johnson, pp. 68-85; and Jane R. Becker, "Auguste Rodin and Photography: Extending the Sculptural Idiom", in Kosinski, pp. 91-115.

Brancusi. Photography, however, was not just a helpful, but humble tool. Rather, for Rodin and other photographically-oriented sculptors, the medium could also serve to redefine sculpture itself by transforming solid, palpable and static matter into an ever-changing illusion or, as Moholy-Nagy put it, into "an almost immaterial substance."[3] Indeed, for some artists, photography seemed capable of liberating sculpture from its very materiality.

Rodin was often actively involved in stage-managing photographic shoots. In the case of Eugène Druet, one of his favourite photographers at the turn of the century, Rodin (who apparently never took a single photograph himself) encouraged his assistant to record works such as the **Eve** from the **Gates of Hell** from the back and side in a mysteriously shadowed, disembodying half-light[4] (cat. nos. 3 and 4). Especially in Druet's back view, the figure of Eve seems to dissolve into her penumbral surroundings, as if on the verge of dematerialising into the 'silence which surrounds things' that Rodin's works evoked for the poet Rainer Maria Rilke.[5]

Or could the incorporeal silence felt by Rilke, who served as Rodin's personal secretary, have been at least partially the result of looking at photographs of the sculptor's figures, rather than at the works themselves? Even more intriguing is the possibility that Rodin himself may have pursued an increasingly dematerialised sculptural style in part thanks to the photographs he encountered, one medium thus reinforcing the aesthetic tendencies of the other. The impact of photographs is incontestable in the case of the writer Charles H. Caffin, who, in 1909, based his reaction to Rodin's controversial statue of Balzac on photographs which captured the "silence [that] renders audible the footfall of incorporeal presences: the shadow seems to be the substance."[6]

The photographs seen by Caffin were the result of a collaboration between Rodin and the young American photographer Edward Steichen. Although Druet had already depicted the **Balzac** as a shadowy figure emerging from the studio's crepuscular darkness, Steichen's roughly-textured prints went even further in

3. Krisztina Passuth, *Moholy-Nagy*, London 1985, p. 306.
4. On Druet, see Varnedoe, pp. 205-206 and 215-224, and Pinet, pp. 76-77.
5. Alex Potts, "Dolls and things: The reification and disintegration of sculpture in Rodin and Rilke", in J. Onians (Ed.), *Sight & Insight: Essays on art and culture in honour of E.H. Gombrich at 85*, London 1994, p. 367.
6. Becker, "Rodin", p. 104.

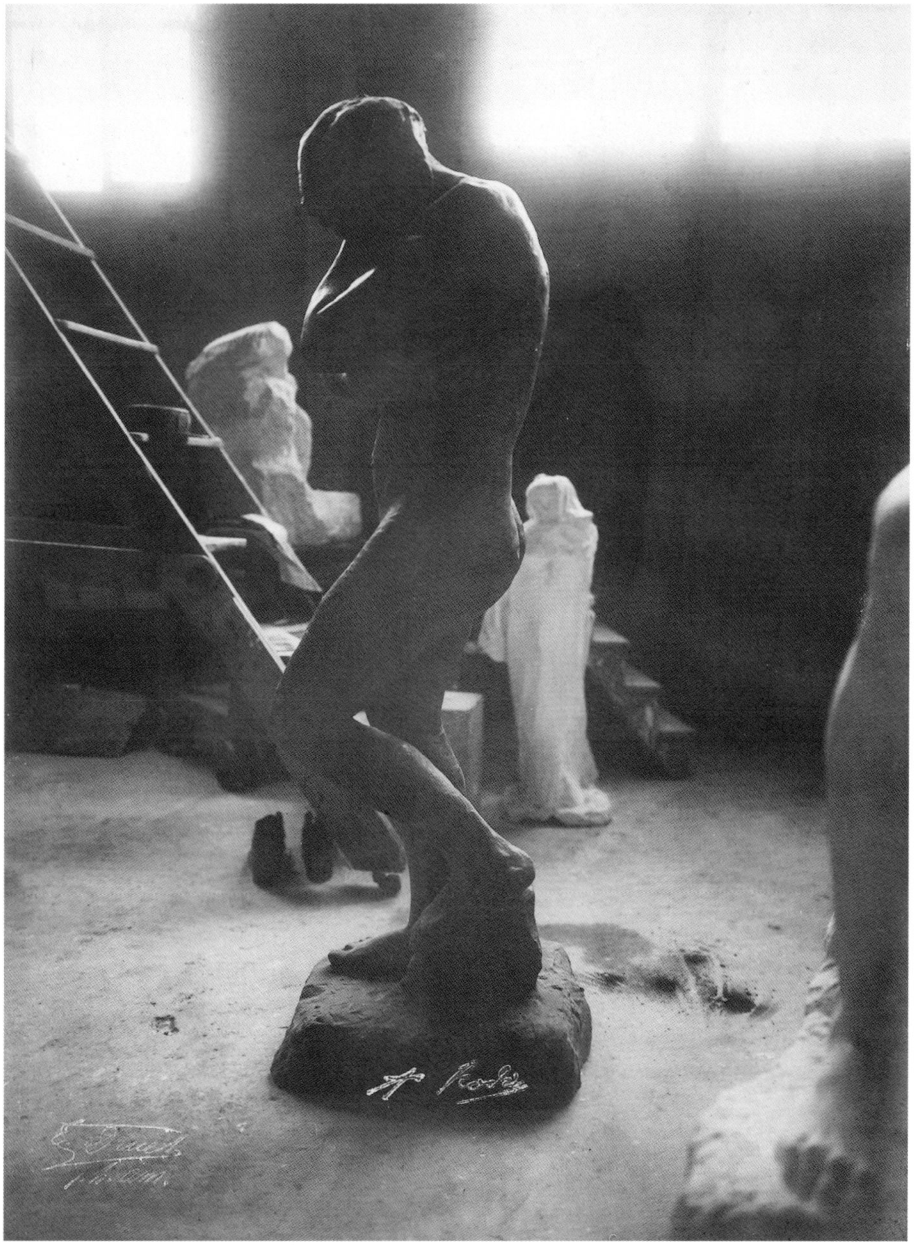

Eugène Druet
Eve
c. 1899 Cat. No. 3

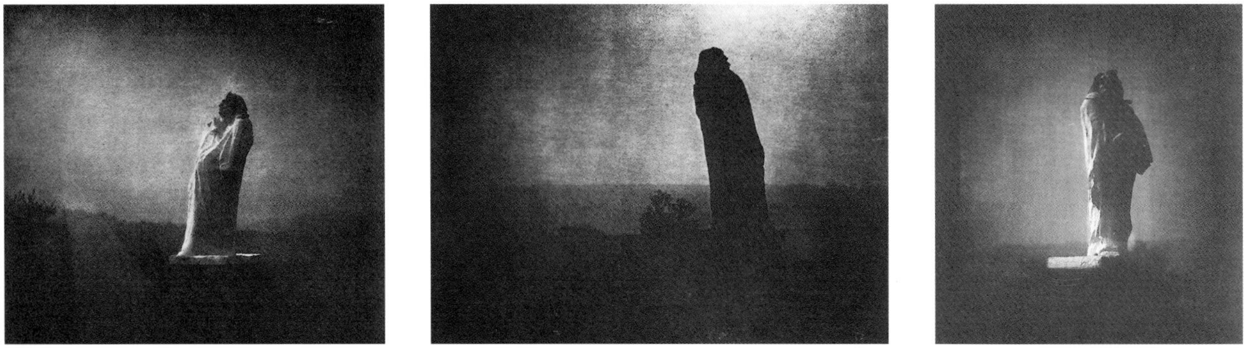

Edward Steichen, three photographs of Rodin's *Balzac*, 1908
(from the left: 'Toward the Light, Midnight', 'The Silhouette, 4 a.m.' and 'The Open Sky').
From _*Camerawork*_, 1911

undermining the fixed, material reality of the statue. Apparently at Rodin's suggestion, a plaster cast of the Balzac was dragged into the garden, set on a rotating platform and photographed by Steichen over the course of two long, sleepless nights. The stunning results were pared down to three key images arranged in a temporal and kinetic sequence running from midnight to dawn and moving around the figure.[7] These images transformed the statue first into a disembodied ghost, then into an inky black silhouette with no recognisable relation to the actual white plaster cast. Photography's ability to transform the very materials of sculpture is also seen in photographs of Rodin's **Burghers of Calais** taken by Jean-François Limet, a studio assistant (cat. nos. 6 and 7). Once again, the slightly unfocused lens and rough surface textures of the prints leave viewers uncertain as to whether the hazy, mysterious figures are cast in dry white plaster or dark gleaming bronze.[8]

The grainy, often technically imperfect and highly atmospheric photographs taken by Druet, Steichen and Limet in many ways recall the unfinished surfaces, purposefully preserved imperfections and serial reworkings that were the hallmarks of Rodin's own sculptural style. Indeed, his obsession with endlessly revising and replicating sculpted works in different media with only slight variations in surface texture and scale found its perfect echo in the disembodied and endlessly mutable figures that populated the photographs he most admired.

7. On these photographs, see Varnedoe, pp. 229 and 235-238.
8. As noted by *Ibid.*, p. 242.

Rosso

At least one disgruntled contemporary was convinced that his own example lay behind the dematerialising tendencies of Rodin's sculptural practices and photographic preferences. Indeed, the Italian sculptor Medardo Rosso became convinced that his 'Impressionist' sculptures in wax, plaster and bronze had inspired Rodin's most innovative works, including the **Balzac**.[9] Rosso and Rodin initially had been friendly, mutual admirers. By 1904, however, six years after the **Balzac's** unveiling, Rosso had had enough. Certain that this statue owed much to his own stylistic proclivities, Rosso assembled a small group of sculptures and photographs for display at the Salon d'Automne in Paris. Amongst the latter were photographs of works by him and by Rodin, including the **Balzac** captured in a deeply shadowed print by Druet.[10] The Italian sculptor's suspicion that his much better-known colleague was appropriating his sculptural strategies without due acknowledgment is suggested by the note Rosso scribbled alongside a photograph of this curious multi-media ensemble: "Confrontation at the Salon, Paris."[11]

Presumably, Rosso believed that a visual (as well as virtual) confrontation with his famous rival effected in large part through the medium of photography would prove his point, namely, that his example had pushed Rodin to develop a dematerialising sculptural style that allowed beholders "to forget matter."[12] However, one could argue that Rosso's sculptural style was itself, to some extent, the product of the dematerialising *photographs* taken of his own works. Although there has been some debate as to whether all the photographs associated with Rosso were actually taken by his own hand, there is no doubt that, unlike Rodin, he was a very active photographer.[13] The resulting images made his already highly-textured sculptures seem to dissolve completely into a misty, nebulous haze.

9. On Rosso, see: G. Moure (Ed.), *Medardo Rosso*, Santiago de Compostela 1996; Jane R. Becker, "Medardo Rosso: Photographing Sculpture and Sculpting Photography", in Kosinski, pp. 159-175; and Harry Cooper and Sharon Hecker, *Medardo Rosso: Second Impressions*, New Haven 2003. I would like to thank Michael Archer for kindly lending me his copy of Moure's catalogue.
10. The Druet photograph is illustrated in Varnedoe, p. 221, fig. 9.28.
11. See Sharon Hecker, "Reflections on Repetition in Rosso's Art", in Cooper and Hecker, pp. 64-67, and Becker, "Rosso," pp. 167-168.
12. Moure, p. 130.
13. On the attribution of Rosso's photographs, see: Luciano Caramel, "Identity and Current Relevance of Medardo Rosso", in Moure, p. 106, and Becker, "Rosso", p. 159.

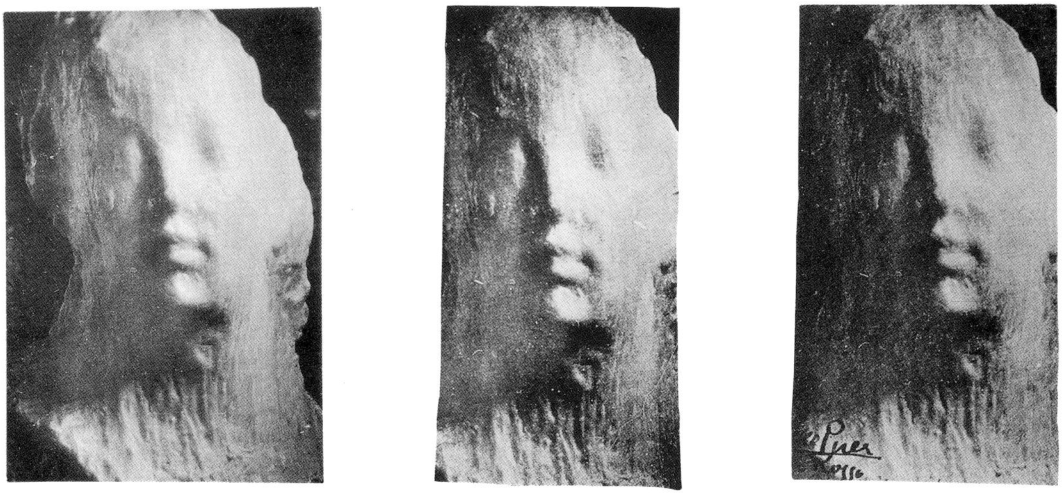

Medardo Rosso (attributed), three photographs of *Ecce puer*, c. 1906. (Museo Medardo Rosso, Barzio)

The photographs taken of Rosso's **Ecce puer** (Behold the child) in c.1906 demonstrate his consciously dematerialising photographic practices, with the prints' technical imperfections mirroring the accidental flaws and blemishes he also relished in his sculpted works.[14] The bust was apparently conceived after Rosso caught a glimpse of a young boy pressing his face through a thin curtain. This fleeting impression of a veiled being is hauntingly evoked by the indistinct surface textures of the sculpture. But the effect is heightened when the bust is seen through yet another veil, that of the photographic medium. Like Rodin, Rosso used dematerialising photographs of such objects to create new, virtual variations of a work that itself had been cast in multiple versions.

At the same time that Rosso's impressionistic photographic style gave him the freedom endlessly to revise sculptural compositions, like Rodin, he too jealously guarded the right to oversee the nature of these variations. Rodin insisted on approving and eventually co-signing all photographs issued by his studio photographers.[15] Similarly, Rosso stated in a letter of 1926: "I cannot allow other photographs to be taken. I want those of mine and no others. I also believe these are the best."[16]

14. On this composition, see Harry Cooper, "Ecce Rosso!", in Cooper and Hecker, pp. 14-15, and Hecker, pp. 51-54.
15. See Elsen, 1980, p. 14.
16. Moure, p. 299.

Throughout his life, Rosso repeatedly claimed that "material does not exist ... Nothing is material in space."[17] However, it was only thanks to his manipulation of the photographic medium that his complex sculpted objects managed to shed their material qualities and be transformed into a series of disembodied 'impressions'. Indeed, it was the shadowy impression of a sculpture, best captured in photographs, rather than the solid, physical object itself that ultimately most fascinated Rosso: "That shadow on the ground is more important than the shoes. So let's deal with the shadow and forget the shoes."[18]

Moholy-Nagy

By the time Rosso died in 1928, photography's ability to materialise the impalpable, while simultaneously dematerialising what was solid and real had fired the imagination of a new generation of sculptor-photographers. One of the most successful in articulating such ideas was the Hungarian artist László Moholy-Nagy.[19] In 1927, he confidently stated that photography gave "tangible shape to light" itself.[20] Moholy-Nagy was well aware, however, that photography could also dematerialise any three-dimensional object it encountered. For Moholy-Nagy, this paradox seems first to have become apparent in 1922 when, in collaboration with his first wife Lucia, he began developing a new photographic technique he dubbed the 'photogram', the "most completely dematerialized medium" (cat. nos. 43-54).[21]

Unlike conventional photography, which relied on light passing through a camera's aperture, a photogram was made by allowing light to strike small, solid objects placed directly on light-sensitive photographic paper.[22] For Moholy-Nagy, photograms effectively gave a fixed, material presence to light itself, while denying the specific materiality of the objects used in the process. Significantly, in a note scrawled on the back of a photogram made in about 1924, Moholy-Nagy stated that

17. For instance, see *Ibid.*, p. 171.
18. *Ibid.*, p. 183.
19. On Moholy-Nagy, see: Sibyl Moholy-Nagy, *Moholy-Nagy. Experiment in Totality*, Cambridge, Mass., 1969; Andreas Haus, *Moholy-Nagy: Photographs and Photograms*, trans. F. Samson, London 1980; Passuth; and Eleanor M. Hight, *Picturing Modernism: Moholy-Nagy and Photography in Weimar German*, Cambridge, Mass., 1995.
20. Christopher Phillips (Ed.), *Photography in the Modern Era: European Documents and Critical Writings*, 1913-1940, New York 1989, p. 85.
21. Passuth, p. 326.
22. On camera-less photography, see: Haus, pp. 13-25; Hight, pp. 57 ff; and Michel Frizot (Ed.), *A New History of Photography*, Cologne 1998, pp. 442-446.

he had used napkin rings and matches to generate the image, then asked: "But is that important in the end? How the light flows ... and what becomes of the whole has nothing anymore to do with the original material."[23] By using multiple light sources when producing a photogram, the silhouetted shape of the 'original material' could be doubled and dislocated, an effect similar to some of the abstract, black-and-white intaglio prints Moholy-Nagy also made in the early and mid-1920s (cat. no. 41).

In his sculptural constructions and mobile multi-media installations, Moholy-Nagy further explored the possibilities of using light as a 'medium of plastic expression' and, conversely, of transforming plastic material into 'light compositions', the latter phrase used in reference to the transparent Plexiglas constructions he produced in 1946, the last year of his life (cat. nos. 57 and 58).[24] Interestingly enough, such complex exchanges between two and three dimensions, between motion and stasis, between transparency and opacity were often realised or at least confirmed through photography and, occasionally, in film, as seen in the case of a rotating sculpture known as the **Light-Space Modulator**, first conceived by Moholy-Nagy in 1922, then photographed and filmed by him when finally completed in 1930.[25]

Gabo

The notion that photography and film can transform the material into the immaterial and back again also permeates the work of the Russian artist Naum Gabo.[26] In the case of Gabo's **Kinetic Construction (Standing Wave)** of c.1919-20, a piece that consists of a vibrating vertical metal rod, Moholy-Nagy observed that a "blurred photograph" of the work showed "several phases of motion superimposed. (What would elsewhere be regarded as an unsuccessful photograph is in this instance a good demonstration of the processes of motion, of the resulting virtual volumes.)"[27] (cat. no. 25). Ironically, these 'virtual volumes' are perhaps *most* evident

23. Katherine Ware, Introduction, *László Moholy-Nagy: Photographs in the J. Paul Getty Museum*, Malibu 1995, p. 12.
24. Passuth, pp. 292 and 383.
25. On this project, see: Rosalind Krauss, *Passages in Modern Sculpture*, Cambridge, Mass., 1977, pp. 206-213; Passuth, pp. 53-56; and Ware, pp. 80-83.
26. On Gabo, see: Steven A. Nash and Jörn Merkert (Eds.), *Naum Gabo: Sixty Years of Constructivism*, Munich 1985; and Martin Hammer and Christina Lodder, *Constructing Modernity: The Art & Career of Naum Gabo*, New Haven 2000.
27. László Moholy-Nagy, *The New Vision: From material to architecture*, trans. D.M. Hoffmann, New York 1932, p. 127.

when looking at a photograph of the sculpture, which permanently fixes the object's full range of oscillation, rather than when standing before the work itself.

From the mid-1920s onwards, Gabo began to use transparent and translucent materials such as Plexiglas and nylon filament in his sculptures (cat. nos. 26-29). These works on the one hand seemed dematerialised due to their lack of solid or opaque surfaces, while on the other hand, allowed light itself to be fixed into a permanent plastic form thanks to the light-'trapping' properties of the reflective materials used. Once again, however, this paradox is perhaps more apparent in *photographs* of Gabo's works than in the physical objects themselves. Especially when photographed against a black background, the bright lines of light that pick out the sculptures' edges, curves and strings seem to reduce the three-dimensional objects to linear tracings that echo his wood engravings[28] (cat. nos. 30-36).

Even more striking are the similarities the prints and the photographs of his sculptures have with photographs taken by Gabo in 1941 of moving, abstract patterns of light (cat. nos. 37 a-e). Already in 1923, Moholy-Nagy had toyed with the idea of photographing light beams projected onto a screen.[29] Gabo was inspired actually to take such photographs in part by his slightly earlier experiments with similarly twisting and curving forms in the translucent sculptures he designed in the later 1930s. The light-photographs, in turn, seem to have given further momentum to his interest in exploring spiral shapes in three-dimensional media in the following years as seen in his **Spiral Theme**, another example of the materialising, dematerialising and rematerialising exchanges that could occur between two- and three-dimensional works of art[30] (cat. no. 28).

Brancusi

While Gabo only occasionally took photographs, the Romanian artist Constantin Brancusi repeatedly photographed his own sculptures and studio environment.[31] Like Rodin and Rosso, both of whom he seems to have known, Brancusi was highly

28. On Gabo's monoprints, see Hammer and Lodder, pp. 328-330.
29. See Haus, pp. 16-17.
30. See Hammer and Lodder, pp. 279-81.
31. On Brancusi as a photographer, see: Marielle Tabart and Isabelle Monod-Fontaine, *Brancusi Photographe*, Paris 1977; Friedrich Teja Bach, "Brancusi and Photography", in F.T Bach, M. Rowell and A. Temkin (Eds.), *Constantin Brancusi: 1876-1957*, Cambridge, Mass., 1995, pp. 312-319; Paul Paret, "Sculpture and Its Negative: The Photographs of Constantin Brancusi", in Johnson, pp. 101-115; and Elizabeth A. Brown, "Brancusi's Photographic In-Sights", in Kosinski, pp. 266-285.

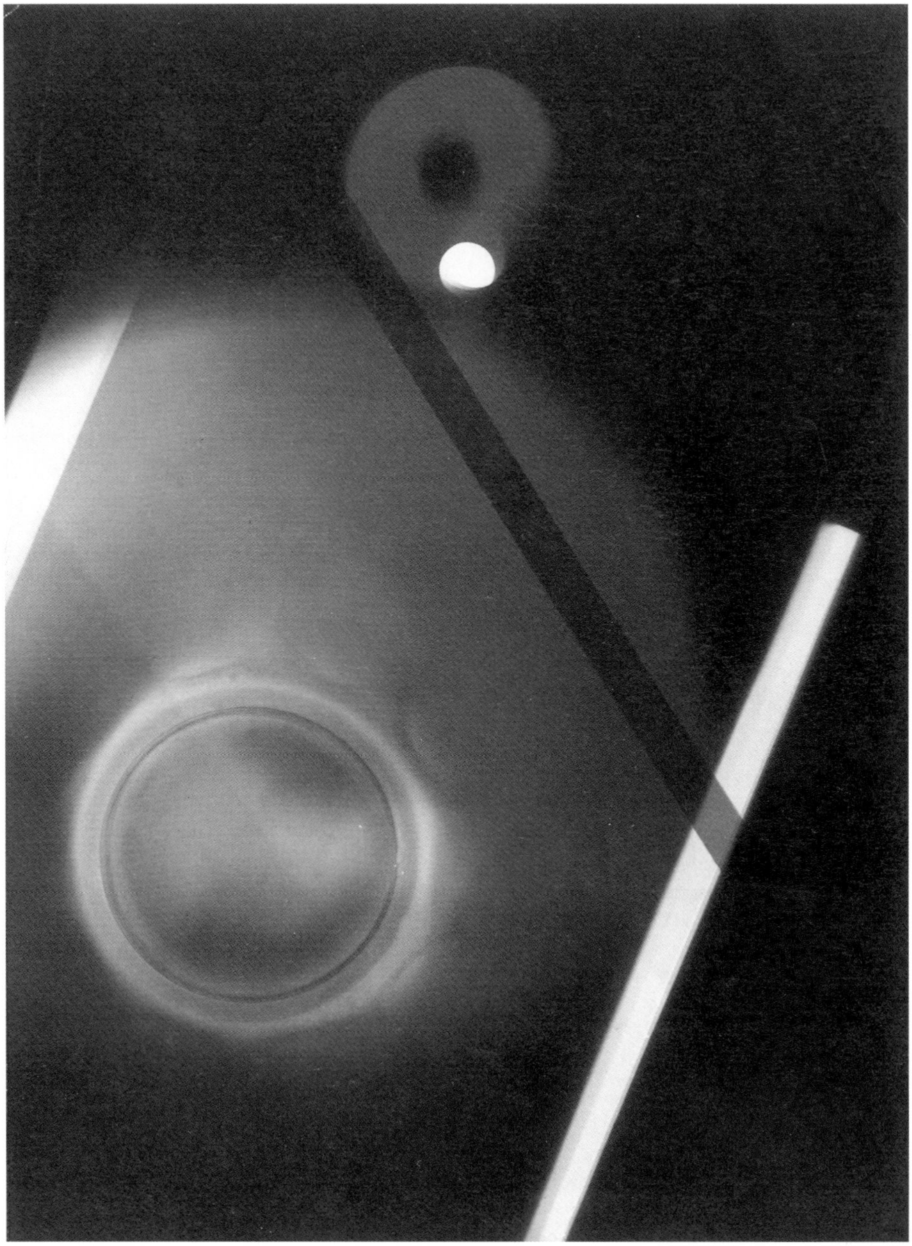

László Moholy-Nagy
Untitled photogram
c. 1922-5 Cat. No. 45

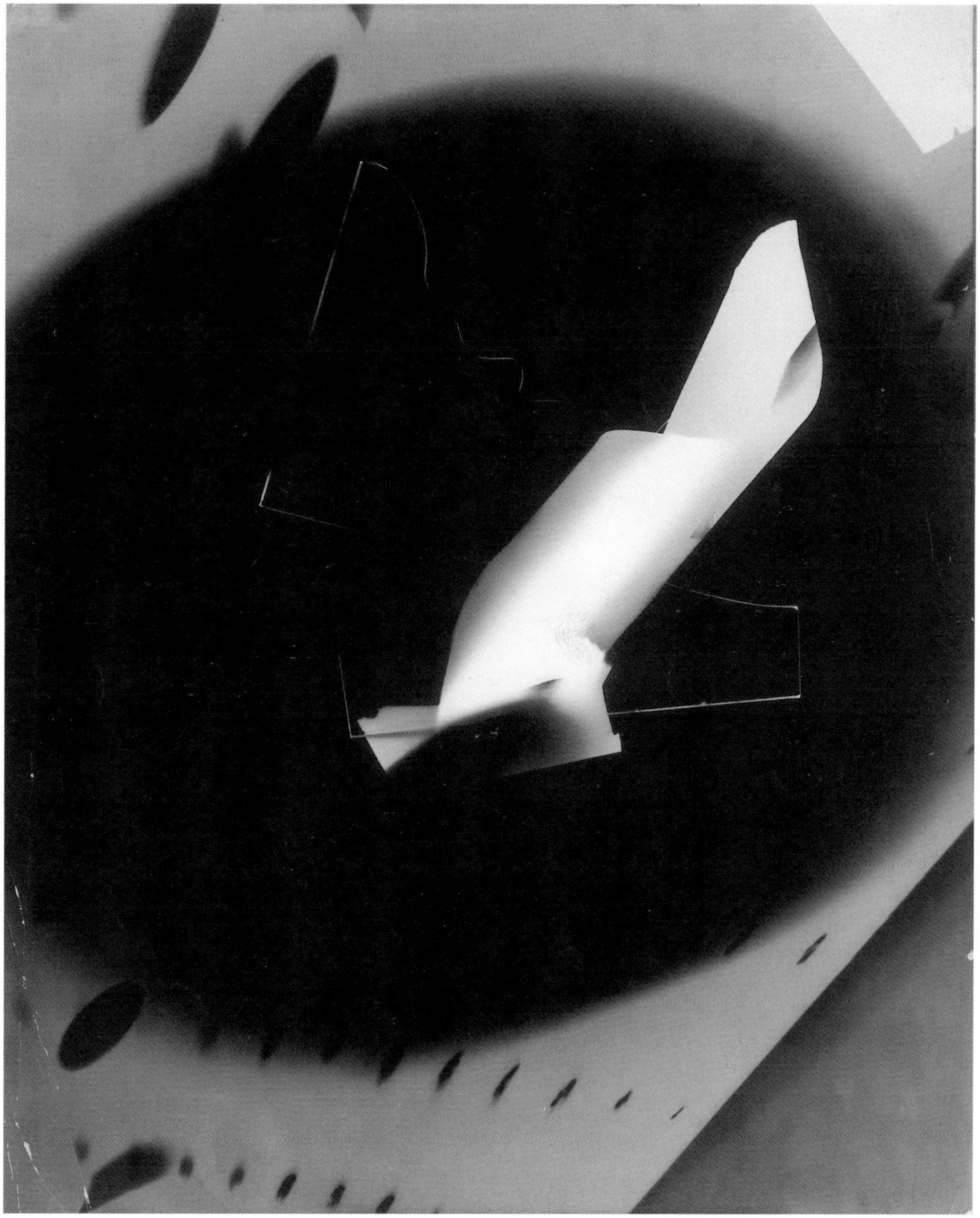

László Moholy-Nagy
Untitled photogram
1939 Cat. No. 56

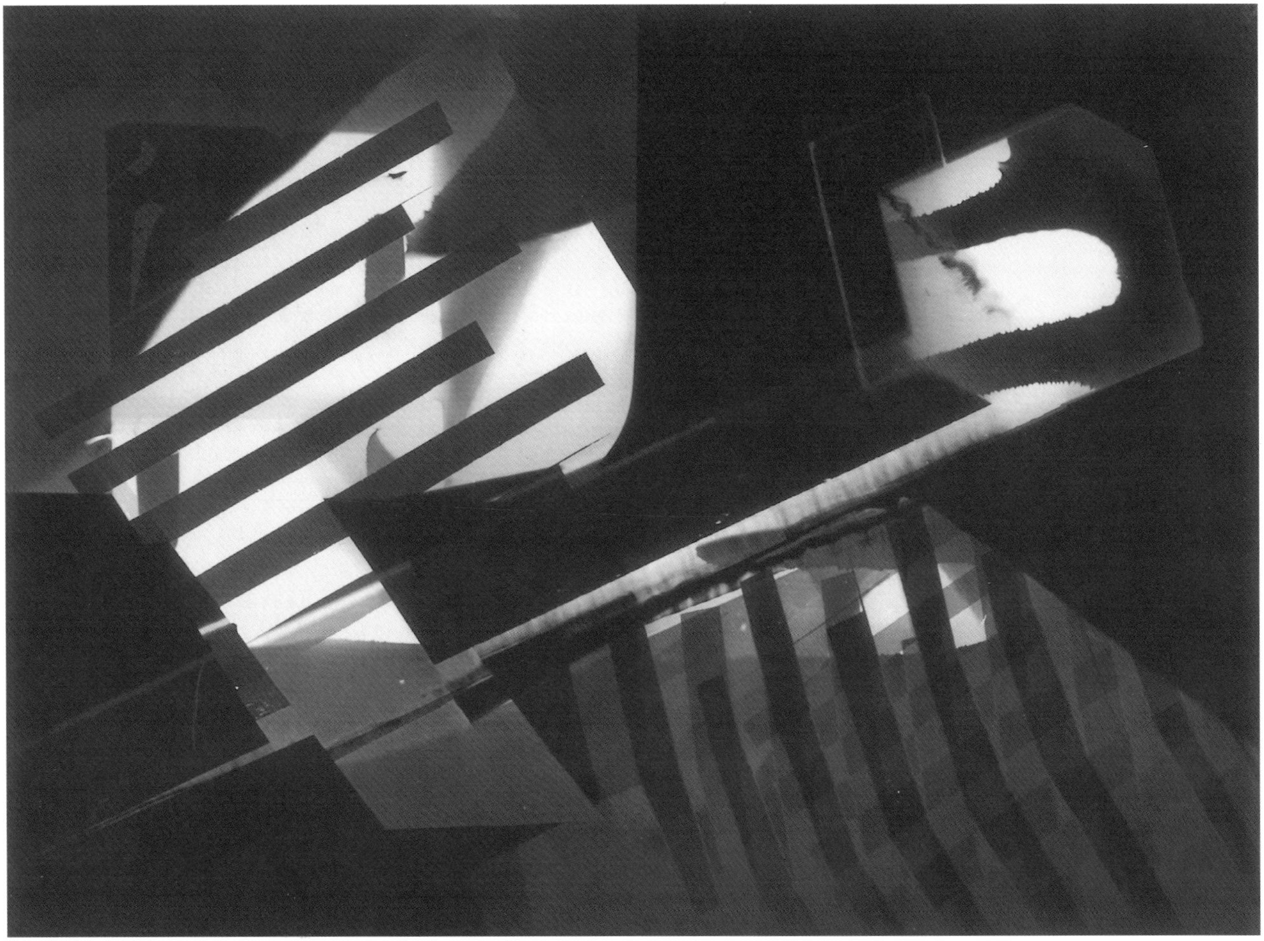

László Moholy-Nagy
Untitled photogram
1923 Cat. No. 46

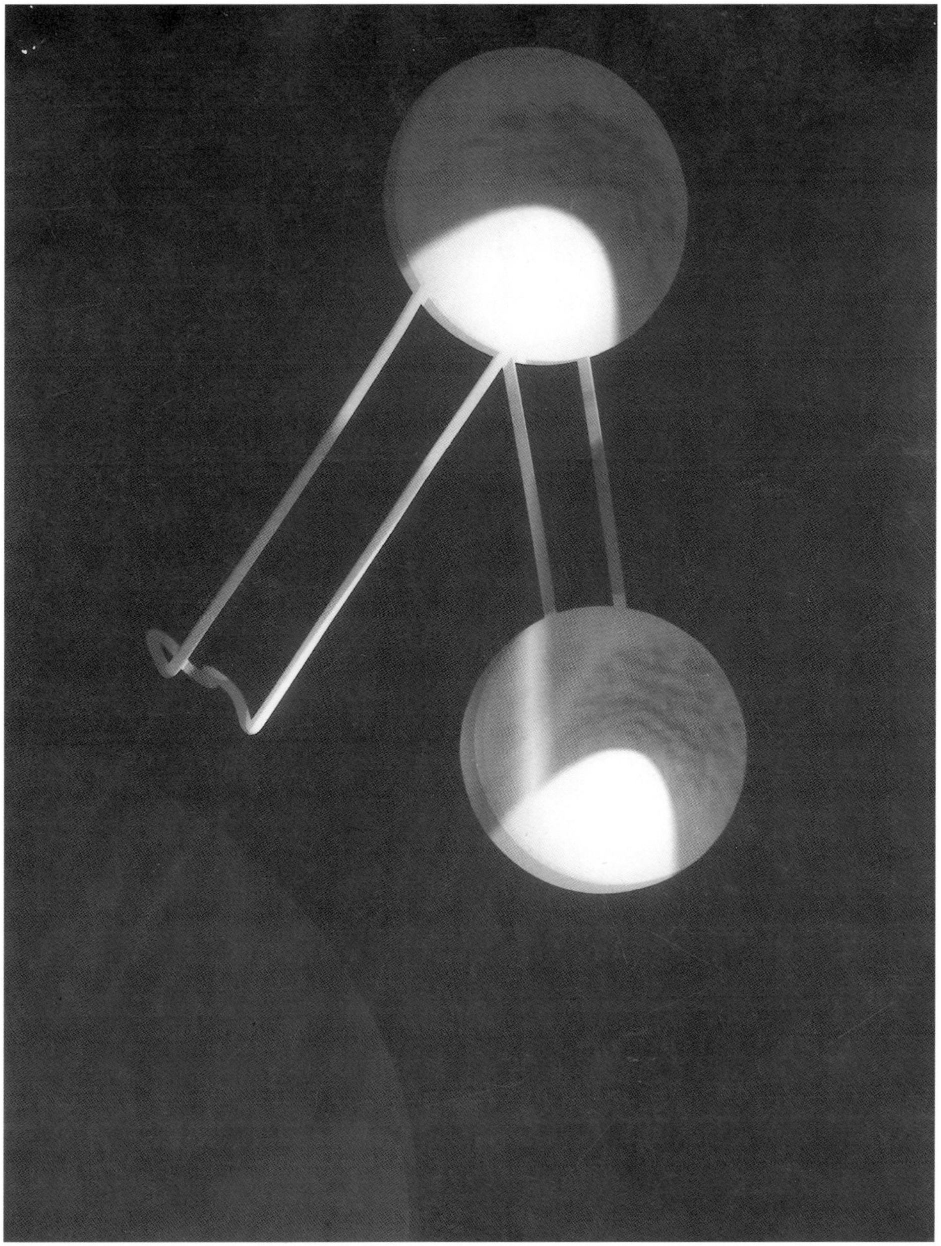

László Moholy-Nagy
Untitled photogram
1925-28 Cat. No. 53

sensitive as to how and by whom his works were photographed.[32] From the 1920s onwards, after seeing photographs by Alfred Stieglitz, Brancusi had insisted that he alone should photograph his sculptures. The artist Man Ray described the defining episode as follows: upon seeing a Stieglitz print of one of his sculptures, Brancusi admitted that it "was a beautiful photograph, ... but it did not represent his work. Only he himself would know how to photograph it .... [The prints he subsequently made] were out of focus, over or underexposed, scratched and spotty. This, he said, was how his work should be reproduced. Perhaps he was right—one of his golden birds had been caught with the sunrays striking it so that a sort of aurora radiated from it, giving the work an explosive character."[33]

The photograph seen by Ray must have been of a bronze version of Brancusi's **Bird in Space**, a composition he repeatedly photographed in the later 1920s and early '30s with 'explosive' bursts of light (cat. nos. 19-23). The photographic imperfections noted by Ray recall the blurred and grainy prints associated with Rosso and Rodin. Unlike these artists' photographs, however, Brancusi's prints were in sharp contrast to the slippery-smooth, glistening surfaces of his actual sculptures. Indeed, **Bird in Space** was so perfectly polished that, in 1926, a U.S. customs clerk had tried to have the piece taxed in the same category as machine-made metal kitchen utensils and hospital supplies.[34] Although the rough and uneven surface effects of Brancusi's photographs seem, at first glance, completely estranged from those of his sculptures, they were both the result of a laborious process of hand-crafting and finishing undertaken by the artist himself.

While most 'professional' photographs of Brancusi's works emphasise their immobile and impenetrable materiality, his own prints make it clear that he did not perceive his sculptures to be stable, solid, static objects. In his photographs of **Bird in Space**, flashes of light dissolve the dense, unitary wholeness of the sculpture at various points along its long, slim shaft (cat. nos. 19, 20 and 22). Another tactic was to use one or two light sources to illuminate the piece and cast shadows, as also seen in Moholy-Nagy's photograms (cat. no. 23, and see nos. 19 and 20). The resulting images could make the actual material object difficult to distinguish from

32. Brancusi may have worked briefly in Rodin's studio in 1907 and definitely exhibited with Rosso in 1906. See Krauss, p. 293, n. 13, and Sidney Geist, "Rodin/Brancusi," in Elsen, 1981, pp. 270-273.
33. Bach, p. 319, n. 19.
34. On this episode, see Anna C. Chave, *Constantin Brancusi: Shifting the Bases of Art*, New Haven 1993, pp. 198-249.

its shadowy and dematerialised *Doppelgängers*. Brancusi printed both 'negative' and 'positive' photographs of this work as well, further disorienting and destabilising viewers.[35]

Brancusi also occasionally deliberately double-exposed photographs, thereby dematerialising his sculptures by making them appear to vibrate in space and time.[36] At first sight, such double-exposures recall photographs taken of Gabo's oscillating **Kinetic Construction**. Now, however, it is the camera, rather than the sculpture, that moves. But in both cases, photography introduces an element of time and a sense of motion into the traditionally monolithic and firmly-fixed art of sculpture. In an echo of Moholy-Nagy's rotating **Light-Space Modulator**, Brancusi displayed a gleaming bronze cast of the **Leda** on a mirrored turntable, effectively doubling the composition, and then filmed and photographed it from various angles (cat. nos. 17 and 18). In using two-dimensional media to dematerialise by visual means a solid, sculpted object, Brancusi thus generated new and ever-changing variations of a work that itself existed in multiple versions.

Conclusion

In 1949, Brancusi asked: "Why write [about sculpture]? ... Why not just show the photographs?"[37] Although all the artists considered here did discuss their work in words, it was often through photographs and, occasionally, film that they most eloquently defined a new kind of sculpture unshackled from the constraints of time, space and materiality. Often using new techniques and unexpected materials in both their sculptural and photographic practices, artists from Rodin to Brancusi skilfully deployed two-dimensional media to rework their three-dimensional compositions, in the process creating dematerialised and constantly-changing versions of their designs while, paradoxically, giving a fixed and permanent form to light, motion and even time itself. Through an almost obsessive desire to control the visual (re)presentation of their work and their inspired use of photographic media, these artists insured that sculpture would no longer be limited to solid, static, impenetrable objecthood, but rather could be magically transformed into 'an almost immaterial substance'.

35. See Paret, p. 106.
36. See, for instance, Bach, p. 355, cat. ill. 191.
37. *Ibid.*, p. 312.

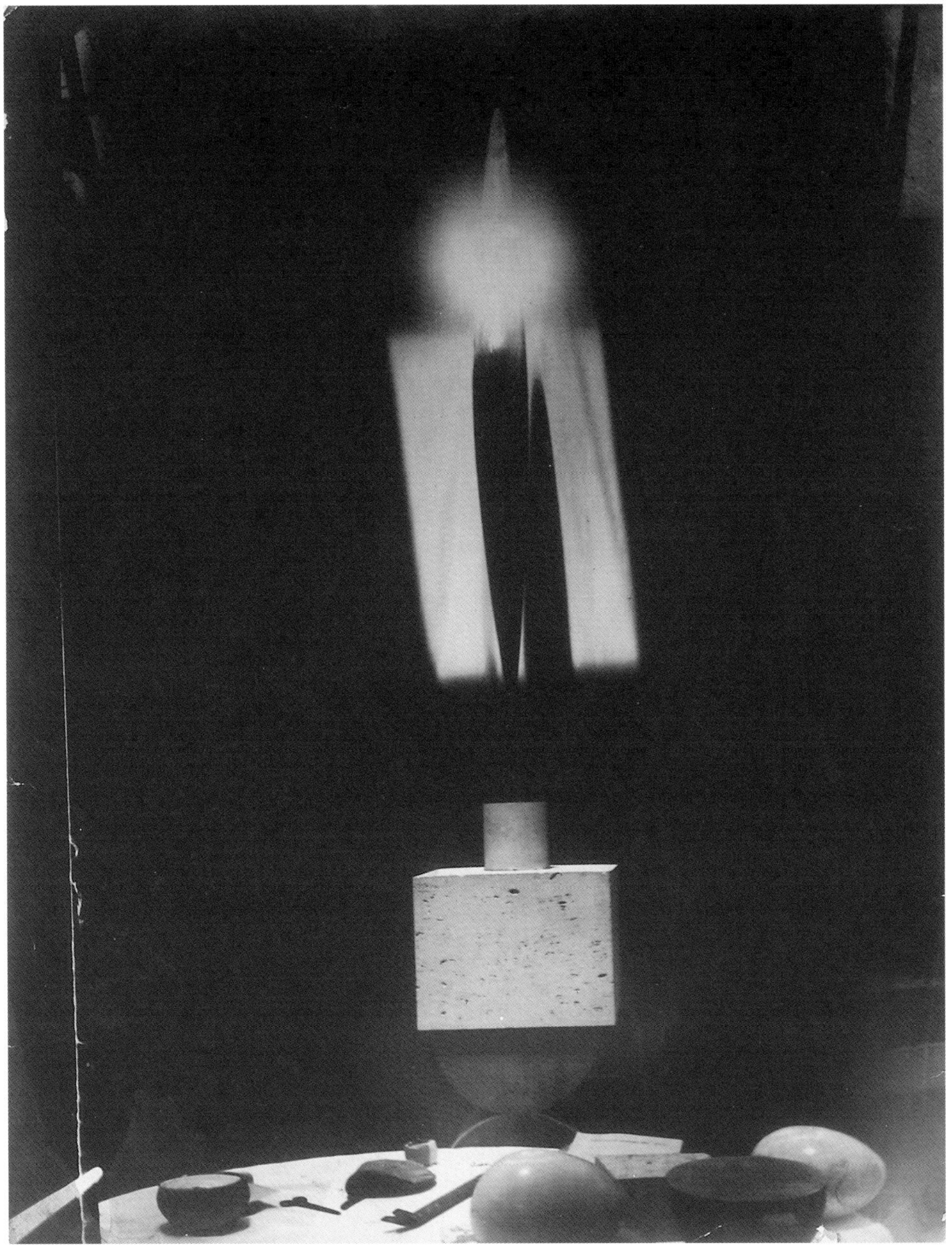

Constantin Brancusi
L'Oiseau dans l'espace (Bird in Space)
1927 Cat. No. 19

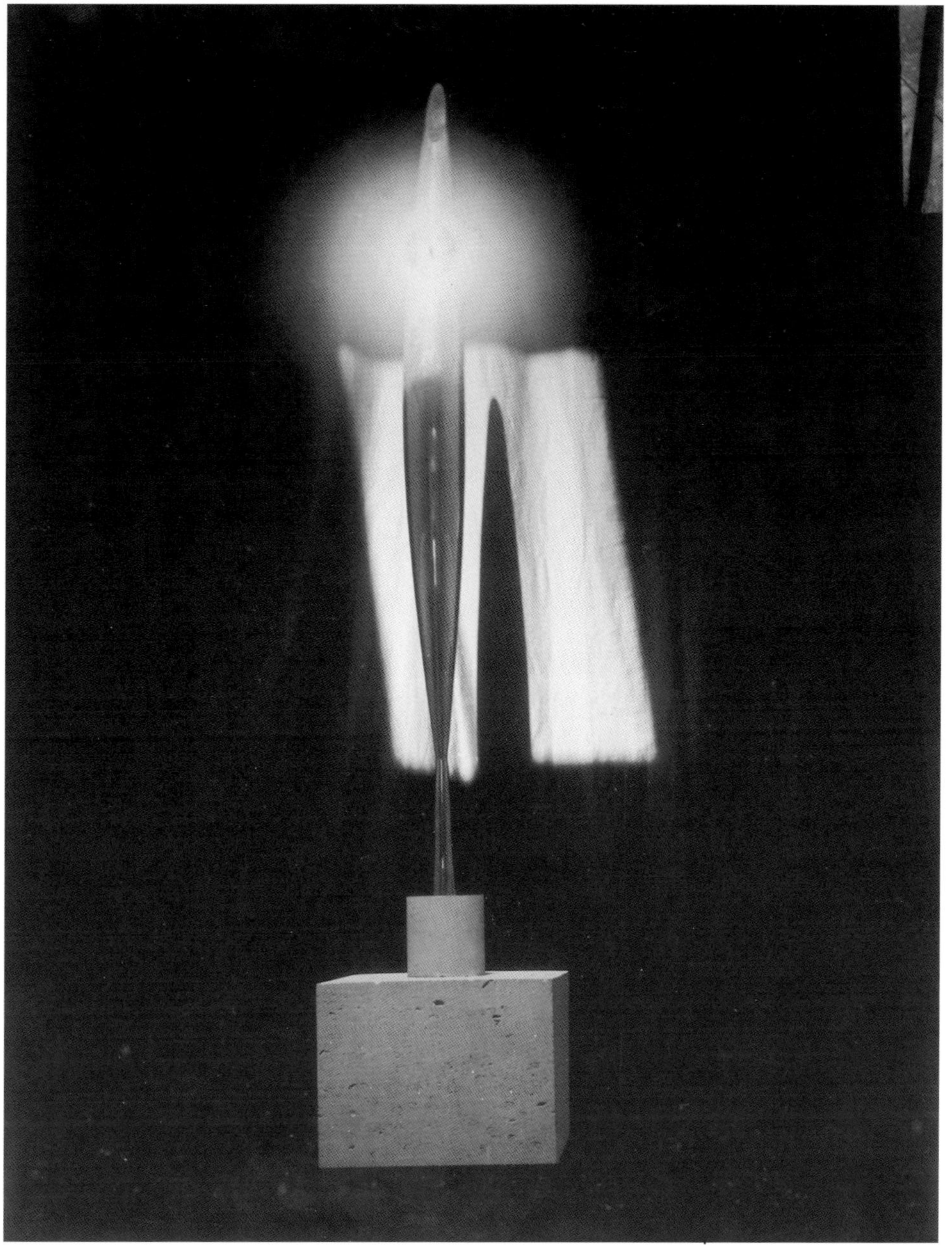

Constantin Brancusi
L'Oiseau dans l'espace (Bird in Space)
1927 Cat. No. 20

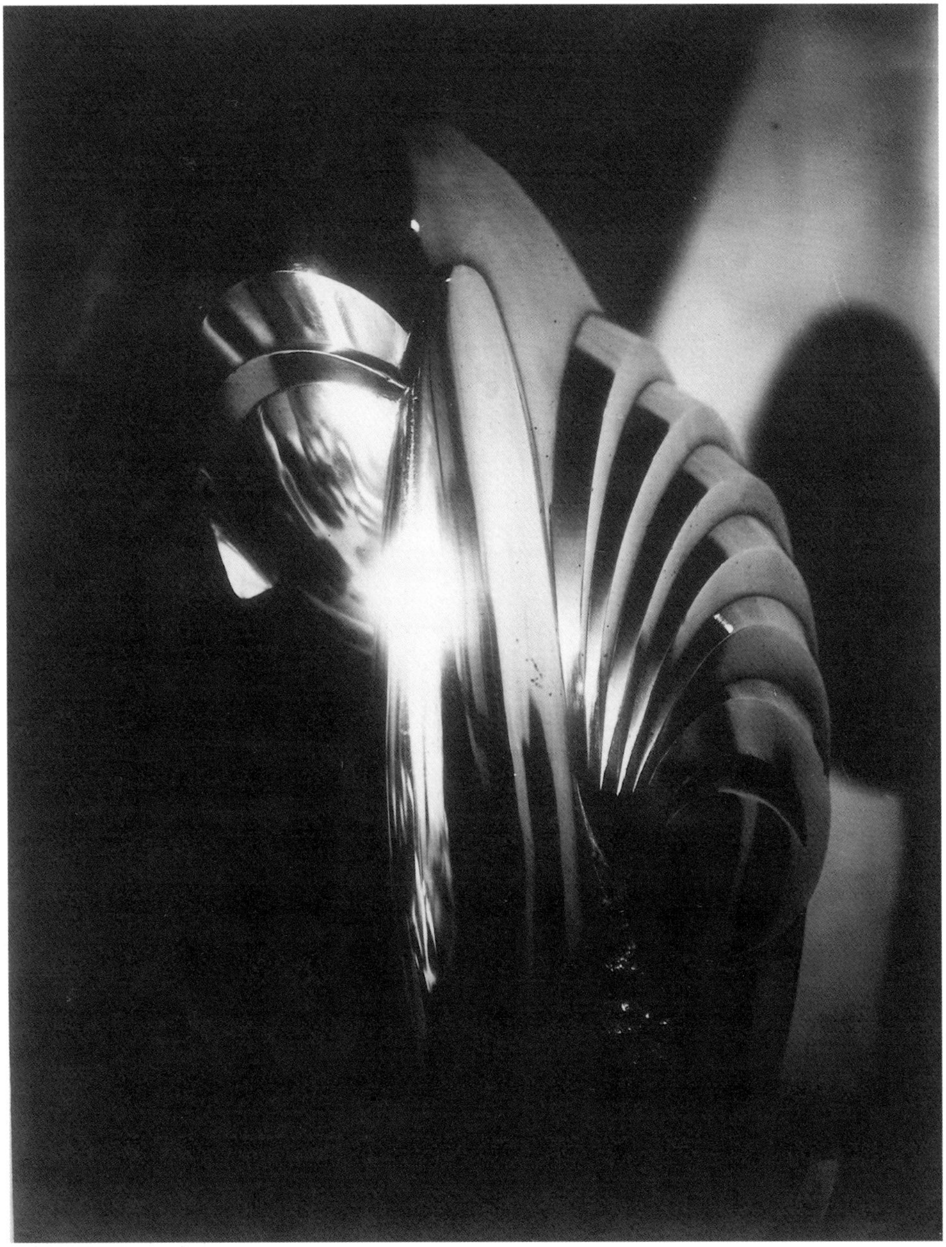

Constantin Brancusi
Mlle. Pogany II
1920 Cat. No. 14

catalogue

Eugène Druet
(1868-1917)

1. **L'Age d'airain (The Age of Bronze)**
   c. 1898
   Gelatin silver photographic print
   39.9 x 29.8 cm
   Musée Rodin, Paris
2. **L'Age d'airain (The Age of Bronze)**
   c. 1898
   Gelatin silver photographic print
   38.8 x 28.8 cm
   Musée Rodin, Paris
3. **Eve**
   c. 1899
   Gelatin silver photographic print
   39 x 28.5 cm
   Musée Rodin, Paris
4. **Eve**
   c. 1899
   Gelatin silver photographic print
   38.8 x 28.5 cm
   Musée Rodin, Paris

Jean-François Limet
(1855-1941)

5. **Le Monument aux Bourgeois de Calais (The Burghers of Calais)**
   c. 1908
   Gum bichromate photographic print
   37.5 x 26 cm
   Musée Rodin, Paris
6. **Le Monument aux Bourgeois de Calais (The Burghers of Calais)**
   n.d.
   Gum bichromate photographic print
   48 x 31.8 cm
   Musée Rodin, Paris
7. **Le Monument aux Bourgeois de Calais (The Burghers of Calais)**
   n.d.
   Gum bichromate photographic print
   28.5 x 39.1 cm
   Musée Rodin, Paris

Constantin Brancusi
(1876-1957)

8. **Prométhée (Prometheus)**
   c. 1912
   Cement
   14.1 x 17.8 x 13.6 cm
   Kettle's Yard, University of Cambridge
9. **Coq (Cock)**
   1924 (cast 1984)
   Bronze
   93 x 10.5 x 38 cm
   Collection Theodor Nicol
10. **Leda**
    1925 (cast 2003)
    Bronze
    55 x 70 x 24 cm
    Collection Theodor Nicol
11. **Poisson (Fish)**
    1926
    Bronze, metal and wood
    93.4 x 50.2 x 50.2 cm (incl. base)
    Tate, London
12. **Prométhée (Prometheus)**
    1911-17
    Gelatin silver photographic print
    23.8 x 29.7 cm
    Centre Georges Pompidou, Paris / Musée national d'art moderne
13. **Mlle. Pogany II**
    1920
    Gelatin silver photographic print
    29.5 x 23.7 cm
    Centre Georges Pompidou, Paris / Musée national d'art moderne
14. **Mlle. Pogany II**
    1920
    Gelatin silver photographic print
    23 x 17 cm
    Centre Georges Pompidou, Paris / Musée national d'art moderne
15. **Mlle. Pogany II**
    1920
    Gelatin silver photographic print
    23 x 17.1 cm
    Centre Georges Pompidou, Paris / Musée national d'art moderne

16. **Leda**
1925-26
Gelatin silver photographic print
17.9 x 23.9 cm
Centre Georges Pompidou, Paris / Musée national d'art moderne

17. **Leda**
1925-26
Gelatin silver photographic print
17.9 x 23.9 cm
Centre Georges Pompidou, Paris / Musée national d'art moderne

18. **Leda**
1925-26
Gelatin silver photographic print
23.9 x 29.9 cm
Centre Georges Pompidou, Paris / Musée national d'art moderne

19. **L'Oiseau dans l'espace (Bird in Space)**
1927
Gelatin silver photographic print
39.8 x 29.8 cm
Centre Georges Pompidou, Paris / Musée national d'art moderne

20. **L'Oiseau dans l'espace (Bird in Space)**
1927
Gelatin silver photographic print
39.8 x 29.7 cm
Centre Georges Pompidou, Paris / Musée national d'art moderne

21. **L'Oiseau dans l'espace (Bird in Space)**
1930
Gelatin silver photographic print
23.8 x 17.8 cm
Centre Georges Pompidou, Paris / Musée national d'art moderne

22. **L'Oiseau dans l'espace (Bird in Space)**
1930
Gelatin silver photographic print
28.7 x 19.3 cm
Centre Georges Pompidou, Paris / Musée national d'art moderne

23. **L'Oiseau dans l'espace (Bird in Space)**
1931-36
Gelatin silver photographic print
17.9 x 11.9 cm
Centre Georges Pompidou, Paris / Musée national d'art moderne

Naum Gabo
(1890-1977)

24. **Model for 'Constructed Torso'**
1917 (reassembled 1981)
Cardboard
39.5 x 29 x 16 cm
Tate, London

25. **Kinetic Construction (Standing Wave)**
1919-20 (replica 1985)
Metal, painted wood and electrical mechanism
61.6 x 24.1 x 19 cm
Tate, London

26. **Construction in Space with Balance on Two Points**
c. 1924 (assembled 1982)
Plexiglas
27 x 37 cm
Nina Williams

27. **Construction on a Line**
1935-37
Celluloid (or Perspex)
45.1 x 43.2 x 89 cm
Tate, London

28. **Spiral Theme**
1941
Cellulose acetate and Perspex
14 x 24.4 x 24.4 cm
Tate, London

29. **Linear Construction No.2**
1970-71
Plastic and nylon filament
114.9 x 83.5 x 83.5 cm
Tate, London

30. **Opus 2**
1950
Wood engraving (monoprint)
20.4 x 15.4 cm
Nina Williams

31. **Opus 2**
1950
Wood engraving (monoprint)
20.4 x 15.4 cm
Nina Williams

32. **Opus 4**
1950
Wood engraving (monoprint)
15.9 x 13.7 cm
Nina Williams

33. **Opus 4**
1950
Wood engraving (monoprint)
15.9 x 13.7 cm
Nina Williams

34. **Opus 4**
1950
Wood engraving (monoprint)
15.9 x 13.7 cm
Nina Williams

35. **Opus 5**
1950
Wood engraving (monoprint)
24.2 x 20.2 cm
Nina Williams

36. **Opus 5**
1950
Wood engraving (monoprint)
24.2 x 20.2 cm
Nina Williams

37. a-e **Five photographs of reflected light pattern**
1941
Modern photographic prints
Various sizes
Tate Archive, London

László Moholy-Nagy
(1894-1946)

38. **Komposition (Composition)**
c. 1923
Linocut
12.1 x 14.8 cm (plate mark)
Cabinet des estampes du Musée d'art et d'histoire, Geneva

39. **Variation**
1924
Woodcut
31.3 x 23.4 cm (sheet)
Cabinet des estampes du Musée d'art et d'histoire, Geneva

40. **Abstufungen (Gradations)**
1924
Lithograph
57 x 37 cm (plate mark)
Hattula Moholy-Nagy

41. **Komposition (Composition)**
1925
Linocut
10 x 12.1 cm (plate mark)
Cabinet des estampes du Musée d'art et d'histoire, Geneva

42. **G 8 (three-dimensional painting)**
1926
Oil on Galalith and cardboard
37 x 46.5 cm
Private collection

43. **Untitled**
1922
Photogram (photosensitive paper, green tone)
30.7 x 23.3 cm
Centre Georges Pompidou, Paris / Musée national d'art moderne

44. **Untitled**
1922
Photogram (photosensitive paper, brown tone)
14 x 9 cm
Centre Georges Pompidou, Paris / Musée national d'art moderne

45. **Untitled**
c. 1922-5
Photogram (photosensitive paper, red-brown tone)
17.9 x 12.9 cm
Centre Georges Pompidou, Paris / Musée national d'art moderne

46. **Untitled**
1923
Photogram (gelatin silver print)
18.1 x 24 cm
Centre Georges Pompidou, Paris / Musée national d'art moderne

47. **Untitled**
1925
Photogram (gelatin silver print)
17.8 x 23.8 cm
Centre Georges Pompidou, Paris / Musée national d'art moderne

48. **Untitled**
1925
Photogram (gelatin silver print)
23.8 x 17.8 cm
Museum Folkwang, Essen

49. **Untitled**
1925-28
Photogram (gelatin silver print)
39.9 x 29.9 cm
Museum Folkwang, Essen

50. **Untitled**
1925-28
Photogram (gelatin silver print)
23.9 x 17.9 cm
Museum Folkwang, Essen

51. **Untitled**
1925-28
Photogram (gelatin silver print)
23.9 x 17.9 cm
Museum Folkwang, Essen

52. **Untitled**
1925-28
Photogram (gelatin silver print)
24 x 17.7 cm
Museum Folkwang, Essen

53. **Untitled**
1925-28
Photogram (gelatin silver print)
23.7 x 17.7 cm
Museum Folkwang, Essen

54. **Untitled**
1925-28
Photogram (gelatin silver print)
20 x 15.5 cm
Museum Folkwang, Essen

55. **Ein Lichtspiel Schwarz-Weiß-Grau (Light Play Black-White-Grey)**
1932
Film
6 mins. 18 secs.
Bauhaus Archiv, Berlin

56. **Untitled**
1939
Photogram (gelatin silver print)
35.5 x 28.2 cm
Centre Georges Pompidou, Paris / Musée national d'art moderne

57. **Leda and the Swan**
1946
Plexiglas
55.9 x 41.3 x 40 cm
Institut Valencià d'Art Modern, Valencia

58. **Spirals**
1946 (replica 1977)
Plexiglas
49 x 37 x 40 cm
Hattula Moholy-Nagy

acknowledgements

The exhibition has been conceived and devised by Sebastiano Barassi, Curator of Collections at Kettle's Yard, and myself. It has been realised with the help of many individuals and organisations.

Our greatest debt is to the lenders, both private and public, who have responded most generously to our requests and allowed us to form the exhibition which we envisaged.

This catalogue is the work of four authors: Christina Lodder and Martin Hammer, whose knowledge of Naum Gabo's life and work is unrivalled, Geraldine A. Johnson, who has made a special study of the relationship between sculpture and photography, and Sebastiano Barassi, whose study of Brancusi and Gabo here at Kettle's Yard has provided the springboard for his essay.

We have received invaluable advice and practical help from Nina and Graham Williams, Hattula Moholy-Nagy, James Hatton (Tate Archive, London), Matthew Gale, Derek Pullen, Jackie Heuman and Catherine Clement (Tate, London), Martin Barnes (Victoria & Albert Museum, London), Belena Chapp (Museums of the University of Delaware), David Juda (Annely Juda Fine Art), Kosme de Barañano and Cristina Mulinas (IVAM, Valencia), Alain Sayag, Doïna Lemny, Lucia Daniel and Darrell Di Fiore (Centre Georges Pompidou, Paris), Hélène Pinet and Sylvester Engbrox (Musée Rodin, Paris), Professor Dr. Hubertus Gaßner and Professor Ute Eskildsen (Museum Folkwang Essen), Cäsar Menz and Nathalie Strasser (Cabinet des Estampes, Musées d'art et d'histoire, Genève), Dr. Peter Hahn and Sabine Hartmann (Bauhaus-Archiv/Museum für Gestaltung, Berlin), Dr Ned Rifkin (The Hirschhorn Museum and Sculpture Garden, Washington D.C.), Charles Pineles (Susse Frères Ltd, Paris and London), Danila Marsure (Museo Medardo Rosso, Barzio), Brian Jenkins (Cambridge University Library) and Mark Nash.

Finally we thank The Henry Moore Foundation and Arts Council England whose grant aid to this project was indispensable, and to the Arts and Humanities Research Board and, again, to the Arts Council for their continuing support.

We are delighted to be working once again with Esta Mion-Jones at Southampton [illegible] bition will have its second showing.